WHAT WOMEN WANT

FUN, FREEDOM AND AN END TO FEMINISM

WHAT WOMEN WANT:
FUN, FREEDOM AND AN END TO FEMINISM

Ella Whelan

Connor Court Publishing

Published in 2017 by Connor Court Publishing

Connor Court Publishing Pty Ltd
PO Box 7257
Redland Bay QLD 4165
sales@connorcourt.com
www.connorcourt.com

Phone 0497 900 685

ISBN: 978-1-925501-47-6

Cover design: Archie Proudfoot

Printed in Australia

Distributed in Australia by Brumby SunState and Connor Court Publishing

Distributed in the UK, Europe, and North America by Ingram Inc.

To my parents, for teaching me to want real freedom

CONTENTS

FOREWORD

I have always felt very privileged to have been born in an era of women's liberation. To live in a time when, in the developed world at least, all members of society, rather than just the male portion, have the chance to unleash their potential.

The liberation of women over the past century from domestic drudgery and the political immaturity imposed on them by a society that didn't trust them to vote, or even to think for themselves, has been one of the greatest gains in the history of humanity.

It hasn't only made society more equal, which is a good in itself, of course; it has made it more energetic, more alive, more intelligent, more thoughtful.

Through welcoming more of the human family — a full half of it — into the worlds of education, work, politics, culture and activism, our societies have made themselves more vibrant. No, not because women bring something special or gender-specific or 'nurturing' to the sphere of public life, but simply because a society that values all of its citizens, rather than just 50 per cent of them, is likely to be a more rounded, fuller and freer one. Through the liberation of women, we have liberated more of the human potential.

And it is precisely because I prize women's liberation so highly that I am concerned about the new feminism.

It is because I value, as all men should, the march of women into public life that I am worried about today's highly fashionable, media-oriented feminism and its promotion of the idea of female fragility.

It strikes me that this new brand of feminism is not harmful to men, as men's rights activists and alt-right keyboard warriors sullenly insist; rather, it is harmful to one of the greatest ideas of the 20th century: that women are just as capable as men of engaging in public life, public debate, politics and work.

Where the first wave of feminism insisted women have the mental and moral wherewithal to be able to vote, and the second wave said women should have the right to work and to be as socially and sexually liberated as (some) men were, the new feminism myopically emphasises women's alleged vulnerability.

It says women are at risk. Words harm them. Insults crush them. Images of naked women damage their self-esteem. Politics is too rowdy for them. The internet is too free-wheeling and unpoliced for women to be able to cope with. 'Reclaim the Internet' is the name of one feminist campaign to make the web a safer — read: more sanitised — space for women.

The terrible irony of this new feminism is that it echoes precisely the attitudes and prejudices that feminism emerged to tackle.

The Suffragettes, and more strikingly their feminist heirs in the confident, exploratory 1920s, rose up against the Victorian view of women as dainty creatures liable to faint upon hearing rough speech. Second-wave feminists challenged the idea that women weren't cut out for work, where they might encounter tension and drama and expletives.

The new feminism seems perversely intent on reversing these victories, through demanding censorship of sexual images, controls on speech, the reshaping of political life to make it more inviting to women, and basically the 'woman-proofing' of public life — that is, sterilising public life to make it safe for ladies.

The problem with the new feminism is that it isn't feminism at all, at least not as we have understood it. Rather, it is shot through with pre-feminist prejudices, though they are now dressed up in the seemingly radical language of 'reclaiming' public life and 'smashing male privilege'. These militant-sounding phrases are a disguise for the cult of vulnerability that feminism has tragically become.

It is little wonder that so few women call themselves feminists (a study in 2016 found that where 85 per cent of Americans believe in women's equality, only 18 per cent of them identify as feminists). This is because the vast majority of women still believe, as do most men, that the so-called fairer sex isn't so fair and can cope with work life and public life as well as any man. One of those women is my colleague Ella Whelan.

Over the past couple of years, Ella has emerged as one of Britain's most trenchant critics of the new feminism and most consistent defenders of the ideal of women's liberation. In the magazine I edit, *spiked*, and elsewhere, she has helped to keep alive the spirit of women's liberation through challenging the treatment of women as victims requiring censorship and authoritarianism to protect them from potential harm.

And now, in this brilliant book, she puts the case for female autonomy against feminist victimhood. Some feminists will no doubt cry 'anti-feminist!', but this would be inaccurate; in fact, this book is in the tradition of the Suffragettes, the female explorers, the female workforce and other female pioneers of the 20th and 21st centuries who demanded that society should mine rather than suppress women's potential. All women and men who value women's liberation should read this.

Brendan O'Neill
Editor, *spiked*

INTRODUCTION

Feminism is back. Forget side-fringes, sportswear and low-slung jeans, feminism is the latest fashion.

From popstars to politicians, over the past five years, female public figures have been keen to sport this latest fashion. 'It's a really ridiculous thing to say you're not a feminist', said the *Twilight* star Kristen Stewart.[1] 'I don't think you can really be a woman in this world and not be [a feminist]', said chat-show host Oprah Winfrey[2]. 'Women saying "I'm not a feminist" is my greatest pet peeve'[3], said vocal US feminist Lena Dunham. Like every other fashion, women who don't wear the label aren't easily accepted by those who do.

Feminism has been portrayed as something as obvious as getting dressed. Of course women are feminists, we're told. Why

[1] Marlow Stern, 'The Resurrection of Kristen Stewart', 10 December 2014, *The Daily Beast* (Online)

[2] Winfrey, Oprah, 'Maker's Profile' (Online)

[3] Mulkerrins, Jane, 'Girls' Lena Dunham: Women saying "I'm not a feminist" is my greatest pet peeve', 14 January 2013, *Metro*, (Online)

wouldn't they be? And it's not just celebrities who have caught on to this trend, or women for that matter. In August 2016, President Barack Obama penned an essay for *Glamour* magazine, on the importance of feminism, writing 'not just as President but also as a feminist'.[4] Back in 2014, the UK cringed as then Labour leader Ed Miliband, then deputy prime minister Nick Clegg and Labour MP Harriet Harman were pictured sporting t-shirts emblazoned with the slogan: 'This Is What A Feminist Looks Like'. (The embarrassment deepened when it was alleged that the t-shirts had been made in a sweatshop.)

The most notable and profligate feminist has to be former US presidential candidate, Hillary Clinton. More than any other public figure, Clinton has encouraged and utilised the resurgence of interest in feminism. Her #GrandmaKnowsBest presidential campaign pushed her gender to attract female voters in what came to be known as 'vagina voting'. In the early stages of her presidential campaign, Clinton was asked in an interview whether she considered herself to be a feminist. She replied: 'Yes. Absolutely. I'm always a little bit puzzled when any woman, of whatever age but particularly a young woman, says something like, "Well, I believe in equal rights, but I'm not a feminist".[5]

Is that what it means to be a feminist today? Simply to believe in equal rights? Is this why so many public figures are backing this abstract political movement? Behind all the grandstanding about feminism, and cries of despair when women decide they won't wear the label, is the idea that to be anti-feminist is to be anti-equality? It seems, that to be anti-feminist is to be anti-woman – to be patriarchal, reactionary and evil.

[4]   Obama, Barack, 'President Barack Obama Says, "This Is What a Feminist Looks Like"', 4 August 2016, *Glamour,* (Online)

[5]   Dunham, Lena, 'The Lenny Interview: Hillary Clinton', 23 October 2013, *Lenny,* (Online)

This book hopes to explain that the opposite is in fact true. That contemporary feminism is a far more complex – and problematic – movement than a simple desire for equal rights. Contemporary feminism is the modern, free-thinking woman's worst nightmare.

From calls to regulate sex and relationships on university campuses to banning adverts for making women feel bad, feminism has become the antithesis of women's liberation. Perpetually portraying women as weak and vulnerable, at every turn, contemporary feminism undermines women's autonomy. The phrase 'strong independent woman', which was brandished with such pride by previous movements for women's liberation, holds no weight with contemporary feminists. Instead, women are encouraged to see themselves as under threat from men, society and even themselves.

This book hopes to reclaim women's autonomy, to wrest back the belief in women's strength and capability from this dire and depressing movement. In revealing how contemporary feminism is failing women, it hopes to inspire a true and meaningful examination of what women want in the 21st century.

Feminism has always asked: What should women be? What should women wear? What should women do? What light should women be viewed in? What identity should women subscribe to?

The only questions this book will ask are: What do women want? What political change do we want to see? What kind of society do we want to live in? What resources do we need to make us truly equal? Unlike its predecessors of the same genre, this is not a do-it-yourself feminist text, a how-to guide on feminism for the under-thirties, or an anecdotal musing on what it means to be a woman. Neither is this book a history of feminism –

there are too many books on that already. Instead, this book is a snapshot of the contemporary moment – it seeks to put women's liberation back on the table and sweep all pretenders to the side.

The next five, short chapters will provide examples of some of the maddest, baddest and saddest campaigns, the worst moments in recent political history for women, and the most threatening moves made by contemporary feminism.

The first chapter examines feminism's disregard for freedom of speech. From online censorship to calls to criminalise wolf-whistling, feminism has become the Mary Whitehouse of the 21st century. Instead of encouraging women to fight back, contemporary feminism calls for the censoring of speech it deems to be offensive to women. In light of the rise in online trolling and panics about gendered language, this chapter will question whether silencing even the most woman-hating rhetoric really benefits women.

The second chapter looks at contemporary feminism's cringe-worthy obsession with the body. Including weight gain, periods, spots and body hair, feminists' teenage obsession with women's bodies has been central to its political outlook. With campaigns showing women standing in their own menstrual blood, revealing their bellies at book signings and stripping naked on protest marches, has feminism become self-obsessed? With campaigns to free the nipple teamed with protests against bare breasts in newspapers, does feminism have an ideal for women's bodies? Are there good ways for women to look at their bodies – and bad ways?

The third chapter looks at feminism's war on sex. Reversing the protests against the *in loco parentis* rules of 1950s college campuses, contemporary feminists are now calling on universities and schools to protect women from men – by limiting alcohol consumption and instituting curfews and segregated spaces. Forget sexual liberation, contemporary feminism's move to police everything from flirting in bars to actual sexual intercourse is a deeply conservative move. Moral panics about a rise in sexual abuse, founded on phoney surveys and scaremongering campaigns, have invited the authorities back into the bedrooms of women. This chapter will look at why contemporary feminists are so down on sex.

The fourth chapter will focus on busting the biggest myth of contemporary feminism: sexism in the workplace. The gender pay gap is feminism's holy grail – a much sought-after fact that is yet to be proven. This chapter seeks to prove that, in 2017, women in the West have never had it so good. But this hasn't stopped politicians and public figures from claiming otherwise. Calls for 50/50 gender quotas and positive discrimination in favour of women utterly degrade any notion of equality or merit. Diversity is now seen as a benefit in itself – an injection of lipstick into parliament is tantamount to a victory for women's freedom. But is this all there is to professional women: the fact that they're female? And does this obsession with equal representation hide a demeaning view of women as in need of a leg-up?

The final chapter asks, do women need feminism? Is this book necessary? The biggest injustice of contemporary feminism is that it's stifling the real fight for women's freedom. Women have it good in 2017, but they could always have it better. Restrictions on women's bodily autonomy and the denigration of women's private lives through state intervention mean that a strong case for women's freedom is sorely needed.

This book rejects feminism, but celebrates women's liberation. It demands our freedom from the state, the authorities and patronising feminists.

1

FEMINISM AND FREE SPEECH

Western women are constantly told that they live in a sexist society. Women are no longer confined to the home, prevented from showing their ankles or even demonised for having a life independent from men. Nevertheless, sexism is apparently rife.

How is this possible? Because today, feminists argue, women are oppressed by words. The more material freedom women gain, the more contemporary feminists want to seek out sexism wherever they can find it. Today, politicians and public figures are not strung up for their policies, or their political plans. More often than not, it will be a comment they once made about women, or a passing joke, that leads to their being put on trial in front of the feminist court.

Back in 2014, self-titled 'pick-up artist', Julien Blanc, was banned from entering the UK and Australia. Blanc became infamous for his lectures to male audiences on how to get girls. His methods were extremely crass and he encouraged his small group of followers to see women as nothing more than notches on a bedpost. Pretty gross stuff from a pretty gross guy. But what was infinitely more disturbing was feminists' reaction to Blanc: they began a petition to stop him from entering their countries.

Forget political debate, ambush, subterfuge or just proving his irrelevance by ignoring him, feminists gave Blanc a gift – they made him headline news. Australian feminist Clementine Ford, who promoted the petition to bar Blanc from Australia, said: 'We're not willing to laugh it off anymore, and in the process we're discovering (once again) just how damn powerful women can be.'[6] In this way, women's power is redefined – it is no longer what we make ourselves. It is no longer about women's ability to change the world around us, but simply our power to pressurise the state to make life nicer for us. In 2015, US rapper Tyler, The Creator was also banned from both the UK and Australia for similar reasons. Contemporary feminists are so unwilling to have an argument, and so hostile to free speech, that they're comfortable with the state banning ideas they don't like.

The Donald

No politician in recent history has said as many crass and ignorant things about women as US president Donald Trump. From calling women fat to infamously suggesting that his favourite dating tactic on a woman was to 'grab her by the pussy', Trump's attitude to women is, to put it lightly, pretty grim.

However, far more gross than Trump's lewd mouth has been the response to his idiotic remarks. High-profile women, celebrities and politicians had a collective public meltdown over the combover wonder. He was branded a danger to women and many feminists argued that his comments alone made them feel physically unsafe. And then, one of the most powerful women in the world, the then First Lady, Michelle Obama, cried, in public, over Trump's comments. 'We have consistently been hearing

[6]   Ford, Clementine, 'Take heart: the tide is turning on sexism and misogyny in Australia', 13 November 2014, *Daily Life*, (Online)

hurtful, hateful language about women – language that has been painful for so many of us', she said[7] in the run-up to Trump's election. Condemning 'vicious language about women', Michelle Obama said of Trump's comments, through tears: 'It is cruel. It's frightening. And the truth is, it hurts.'

After Trump was elected in November 2016, a blog called *Hollywood Life*[8] reported: 'There was a sound rising around the country that was just as loud as the cheers of the Trumpsters. It was the sound of women sobbing.' Crying, sulking, emotional women – that was the image many feminists adopted during and after Trump's presidential campaign.

Following Trump's inauguration in January, there were mass protests, with women worldwide giving the bronze megalomaniac the two fingers. But the message behind these marches was a sense that women were under threat. The organisers of the 'Women's March' released a public statement which read: 'The rhetoric of the past election cycle has insulted, demonised, and threatened many of us.'[9] Trump's words, alone, have apparently made grown women feel threatened. During the protest, women held up signs that said 'we're dying' and 'Trump is evil'. There was no sense that the president should be scared of people power – the protests were no threat to Trump. Instead, some women seemed content to be marching as victims at the hands of a man who had yet to do anything other than be crude about women. From the off, the protest against Trump and his supposed sexism has admitted defeat. If we're reduced to tears by Trump's words, how do we expect to mount a campaign when he acts against women's freedom?

---

[7]   Obama, Michelle, 'The full transcript of Michelle Obama's powerful New Hampshire speech', 14 October 2016, *Guardian,* (Online)

[8]   Fuller, Bonnie, 'Young Women Are In Tears After Donald Trump Is Elected President – Here's Why', 11 November 2016, *Hollywood Life,* (Online)

[9]   'Mission and vision', *Women's March on Washington,* (Online)

Herein lies feminism's biggest problem: it encourages women to be afraid of words. No longer do feminists shout back at unsavoury or insulting comments. Instead, they call for censorship. In the past, women organised and fought sexism to change society's perception of women as weak and childlike. Women are taken seriously because they proved that they can be as tough and ugly as men if need be. Today, this hard-nosed defence of women's independence is being outsourced to external authorities. No one should be allowed to say rude things about women, feminists argue; we shouldn't have to deal with such comments and instead the state should simply make them illegal.

The criminalisation of cat-calling

In Trump, feminists found their real-life sexist bogeyman. But way before Trump was dominating headlines, feminists were waging a war on words. In the UK, in July 2016, Nottinghamshire police reported that they would extend the definition of hate crime in the area to include 'misogyny'. The chief constable, Sue Fish, claimed that criminalising misogyny would make 'the county a safer place for women'. Nottinghamshire has never been a dangerous place, for women, or men. Nevertheless, Nottinghamshire police will now investigate 'incidents against women that are motivated by an attitude of a man towards a woman and includes behaviour targeted towards a woman by men simply because they are a woman'.[10] Translated, this means that anything a man does towards a woman that she doesn't like can be considered a hate crime. This includes rude comments, wolf-whistling and inappropriate questions.

This is shocking. In the UK, right now, a man can be investigated

[10]   Mackenzie, Jean, 'Misogyny hate crime statistics revealed', 19 September 2016, BBC, (Online)

by the police for wolf-whistling at a woman on the street. He doesn't have to touch her, or even speak to her — just making a noise could get him in trouble with the law. The labelling of such minor acts as 'misogynistic' is extremely problematic. Misogyny is defined as a hatred of women. It's the kind of term you use for a serial abuser, someone who doesn't just think women are unequal, or who has a few outdated views about making sandwiches, but who actually *hates* women. The idea that this prejudice is so commonplace it must be outlawed is ridiculous.

And yet, feminists celebrated the overreach of the Nottinghamshire police. Laura Bates, author and founder of the Everyday Sexism movement, praised the decision, demanding that it shouldn't 'simply be a one-off push — it must be sustainable and ongoing'[11]. It's not surprising that Bates and fellow feminists support this law change — they need the panic over 'misogynistic abuse' to continue. In order for the law to be 'sustainable and ongoing', so must the so-called abuse.

There is no real drive here to make any meaningful change. Even if a few guys shouting 'alright sexy' was an issue serious enough to involve the police, feminists aren't interested in how best to stop it from happening for good — they simply want to know that the right measures are in place to 'challenge the normalisation of misogynistic abuse'. These feminists want the police to provide constant surveillance of public interaction in order to protect women. Are women supposed to welcome being watched by the state? Have feminists completely given up on women's capabilities to challenge ideas and speech they don't like?

By making misogyny a hate crime, Nottinghamshire police

---

[11] Bates, Laura, 'Six things we've learned about misogyny as a hate crime', 22 September 2016, *Guardian*, (Online)

have put women into a special category. Women are now seen as a protected group under the law – which inherently means that they're not equal to men. This move suggests that women need special protection, that a woman shouldn't shout back at a guy who says something to her on the street. Instead, she should run crying to the police. This development shows that feminists deem women too weak to handle words. Men are now at risk of criminalisation for saying a duff line, or cat-calling someone in the street. But women are the real losers here, for this law insinuates that they need the authorities to police everyday life on their behalf.

The problem is that what is deemed 'hateful speech' is completely subjective. In 2015, Prince Charles was called out for referring to Camilla, his wife, as 'the missus'. This was considered to be offensive, not because of Charles' faux working-man lingo, but because the word 'missus' is supposedly sexist. Also in 2015, the British scientist Tim Hunt was publicly hounded, and eventually sacked, for a joke he made about female scientists being prone to crying and distracting their male colleagues. Every feminist media commentator raged against Hunt's joke, he was decried as a gross sexist and had his reputation ruined. Eventually, the transcript of the speech was released, revealing that he had not only acknowledged the fact that he was joking, but had continued to praise female scientists.

In Australia, the chair of the diversity council Australia board, David Morrison, launched an embarrassing campaign called #WordsAtWork, denouncing the use of the words 'guys' and 'girls' in the workplace as discriminatory. 'Gender-based language' is 'blatantly inappropriate', he said.[12] This is what happens when you pose women as victims of language; it is the logical point

---

[12]   Greene, Andrew, '#WordsAtWork: David Morrison wants Australians to stop saying gender-based terms like "guys"', 1 June 2016, ABC, (Online)

of feminists' panic about sexist words. Morrison, an old white guy, the stereotypical figure of hatred for feminists, is peddling feminists' own mantra: words hurt women.

It's not just outdated words or unfortunately timed jokes that catch the ire of contemporary feminists. Perfectly normal, everyday words are being held up as problematic. The word 'bossy' has gotten a bad rap recently, with public figures like Michelle Obama getting behind the US campaign to 'Ban Bossy'. What's wrong with the word bossy? According to the campaign, "bossy" is 'a precursor to words like "aggressive", "angry", and "too ambitious" that plague strong female leaders'. Instead of being encouraged to stand up for themselves in the face of criticism, feminists want to protect girls from hearing words that might be critical. So much for nurturing strong, independent young women – these days, feminists are content with portraying women as in need of protection from hurtful words.

No one wants to live in a society which encourages abuse or harassment of women. But the fact is, through the struggles and political battles of women in the past, we don't. In the West, women do not have to walk down the street to the tune of cat-calls and sexually suggestive questions. We don't have to think twice about wearing short skirts and make-up on nights out. There are still some men who will shout something crude, but these instances are rare. Contemporary feminists want to make it seem like women face sexism every time they leave the house. What purpose does this falsehood serve? In branding women as victims, we make it harder to form a serious and forceful political argument. Women should feel empowered to stand up for themselves when a guy wolf whistles and they don't feel like ignoring it – they should feel strong and capable enough to tell that guy to get stuffed. Because who will fight for women's freedom if women themselves won't step up to the plate and make a case for themselves? The reliance on the state and the police is detrimental to women's liberation – it poses us as weak and needy, rather than a force to be reckoned with.

The porn panic

This drive to protect women from dangerous or unpleasant words and images really kicked into gear during the backlash against porn in the 1980s. Feminists' call to ban porn was a graphic example of the shift in tack towards a conservative notion of women as being in need of protection.

Two anti-porn American feminists spring to mind: Catharine MacKinnon and Andrea Dworkin. Both Dworkin and MacKinnon, through the narrative of protection and saving women from sexual abuse, called for the policing and outlawing of pornography. They argued that porn was more than just words and pictures, that it was the physical expression of women's oppression. In *Only Words*[13], in 1993, MacKinnon wrote that 'not only is pornography more than mere words… the power of pornography is more like the power of the state'. Pornography was women's oppression writ large, on the big screen. It wasn't just gross, it was dangerous. MacKinnon and Dworkin called for a law which would make 'graphic sexually explicit materials that subordinate women through pictures or words' illegal.

Acknowledging the argument against her, MacKinnon is defensive. She argues that far from the call to criminalise porn being an act of censorship, rather, it's rather a preventative act – stopping porn will stop sexual abuse.

---

[13]   MacKinnon, Catharine, *Only Words*, 1993, Harvard University Press

Of course, both MacKinnon and Dworkin were not focused on stopping acts. It was words and images that they wanted outlawed. Battery, rape and harassment were already illegal — what anti-porn feminists were really arguing for was an extension of what these categories entailed.

Take this passage from *Only Words*, which almost reads like a university campus policy on sexual harassment from today:

> *If ever words have been understood as acts, it has been when they are sexual harassment. For fifteen years, unremitting pressure for dates, unwelcome sexual comments, authoritative offers to exchange sex for benefits, and environments permeated with sexual vilification and abuse have been legally actionable in employment and education. Only words — yet they have not been seen as conveying ideas, although, like all social practices, they do: ideas like what men think of women, what men want to do to women, what women should do for men, where women belong.* [14]

MacKinnon argues that protecting pornography means protecting sexual abuse as speech — in doing so, she draws a parallel between words and acts: women are physically oppressed by men watching porn.

Dworkin and MacKinnon's argument has inspired several movements against sexualised images of women. For years, feminists campaigned to censor the press and remove the so-called 'Page 3' girls from UK tabloid the *Sun*. Alongside the 'No More Page 3' campaign were even more prudish calls to put lads' mags and other adult magazines in 'modesty bags'. Several universities in the UK have policies which ban lads' mags from campus.

The thing is, this panic about naked women in print is not

[14]   *Only Words*, Pg 45

intended to combat any alleged mistreatment of women in the making of such magazines. It's rather for the protection of the girlfriends of men who read them, or the women who walk past them in the shopping queue. The harm done by explicit pictures of women is felt by women who simply see the magazines, not those whose bodies are used for the photos.

It is in this way that the anti-porn movement has directly influenced the censorious nature of feminism today. In banning lads' mags, student feminists have taken Dworkin and MacKinnon's understanding of pornographic words and pictures, as being equally as damaging as the actions behind them, even further. We shouldn't ban porn because women are exploited in its creation, we're told, but because women who see the magazines get hurt.

It was for this reason that Nadine Strossen, a leading civil libertarian and feminist who wrote *Defending Pornography*[15] in 1995, in response to the anti-porn hysteria. Talking to the online magazine *spiked* last year, Strossen said that, at the time, there was an 'odd alliance between the extremely left-wing anti-pornography feminists and the so-called religious right'.[16] This alliance, based on a desire to protect women from rude pictures as well as a hostility towards free speech, made feminists like Strossen balk. In *Defending Pornography*, Strossen makes the case for an anti-censorship, pro-sex feminism. She quotes women's rights attorney Kathleen Peratis: 'If you love freedom and like sex, censorship is bad news.'[17] This is a mantra all contemporary feminists should seriously consider adopting.

---

[15] Strossen, Nadine, *Defending Pornography*, Abacus, 1995.

[16] spiked podcast, 'Banning pornography is demeaning to women', 29 April 2016, *spiked*, (Online)

[17] *Defending Pornography*, Pg 34

Pornography is a gross pastime. Most women will feel uncomfortable learning that their partners have watched pornography, not because it reveals some innate hatred of women or sexist desire, but because it isn't real life. Pornography doesn't depict real sex, and as such it sucks the meaning and life out of proper sexual encounters. It degrades women but also sex itself – it makes the viewer passive and removed from a feeling that should be real and active rather than staged.

Yes, porn is creepy – but it shouldn't be banned. Not least because adults should be able to look at what they want, no matter how grotesque. Consenting women should feel free to work in the pornography industry if they want to. But most importantly, calling for a ban on pornography is inviting the state into our innermost private sphere – our sexual lives. By inviting the policing of sex in this way, anti-porn feminists planted the idea that women need the state to protect them from men. It insinuated that women can't change culture or ideas or perceptions of themselves on their own. Instead, they must make all depictions they don't like illegal – in order to steer men in a certain direction. In MacKinnon's mind, that is to condition men *not* to rape. But in reality, it is conditioning society to view women as in need of protection by the state – an idea infinitely more dangerous than a seedy film.

The internet
Nowhere has this move to infantilise and degrade women been more pronounced than on the internet, through the panic about internet sexism. Feminists tell women that the internet is a hotbed of sexist rhetoric and that women are constantly at risk from online abuse. In May 2016, UK Labour MP Yvette Cooper set up 'Reclaim the Internet', a cross-party campaign to tackle

sexism online. '40 years ago, the "Reclaim the Night" campaign was launched to build a movement against harassment, abuse and violence against women on the streets. Now the internet is our new streets and everyone should be able to feel safe and speak out online'[18], the campaign states. Apparently, sexism against women hasn't actually been defeated, men haven't changed their views about women. In other words, the feminist movement didn't work. No, apparently all these horrible and abusive ideas about women have simply moved online, the net is the new street, and a nasty tweet is the new sexist abuse.

Cooper has been supported by various MPs, think tanks and organisations. Jess Phillips, another Labour MP, said she supports the campaign because: 'I want spunky women shouting up and facing honest to goodness debate and challenge. Not men with spunky names bullying women into silence'.[19] Rather than encourage women to challenge their detractors, so-called feminist MPs call for the state to remove anything that might inhibit women from speaking up, clearing the path for them to voice their opinions without contestation.

This is the perfect example of feminism's disdain for free speech. 'It's possible both to champion freedom of speech and argue for greater responsibility from everyone', the campaign claims. But if free speech is to be genuinely free, it must be absolute, with no ifs or buts. If it's not absolute, then it's not free speech: it's privileged speech. What the Reclaim campaign is really saying is, 'Yes, free speech for vulnerable women, but not for people who will disagree with our views'. In other words, in the interest of protecting free speech, we must limit it. Are women really comfortable with this?

[18]   Reclaim The Internet (Online)

[19]   Phillips, Jess, 'Reclaim the Internet – Fighting for Freedom of Speech', 25 May 2016, *Huffington Post,* (Online)

The bizarre idea that it is possible to expand freedom of speech by limiting it involves identifying those groups that have the ability to speak freely and those that do not. The argument often made by censors is that by stopping one group from talking so much, you allow another group to get a word in edgeways. Black is white, good is bad, censorship promotes freedom of speech.

The idea that minority groups and women need to be protected from online speech is not only patronising – it's also untrue. Indeed, a large proportion of internet trolls are reportedly young women – supposedly the most vulnerable of all the victim groups. A report by the think tank Demos gave evidence that over 50 per cent of misogynistic comments made on Twitter were from women.[20] By cloaking a serious threat to free speech in the language of victimhood and protection, Cooper's campaign has succeeded in obscuring what is really going on here. In the name of protecting women and minority groups, the Reclaim campaign is attacking our right to free expression. 'We're calling for your views on what more the police and prosecutors should be doing', Cooper wrote in the *Telegraph*.[21]

The idea that women need loud, brash men to be silenced in order to unleash their full potential online represents a damning view of women – just like the suggestion that black people need (still overwhelmingly white) authorities to make the internet a Safe Space for them. Everyone knows that Twitter is a hotbed of kneejerkers and troublemakers. Our message to shrinking violets should be: if you don't like it, stay away from it. There is no social obligation to tweet. We should also defend the right to get angry; the freedom, that is, to let a few expletives end a boring online

[20] *Demos*, 'The Use of Misogynistic Terms on Twitter', 26 May 2016 (Online)

[21] Cooper, Yvette, 'Why I'm campaigning to reclaim the internet from sexist trolls', 26 May 2016, *Telegraph*, (Online)

argument. Do women really want to take the emotion out of public discussion for the sake of a few hurt feelings?

The answer is, of course, no, women have never called for such regulation and protection in their personal lives. There is no national movement in the UK to clamp down on free speech in the name of protecting women. Most women recognise that there will always be mean and rude people in the world. As the panic about sexism online reaches new heights, those who do want to cause trouble tend to go for what they know will get a reaction. There's no better way of upsetting a feminist than telling her to go make you a sandwich. Trolls and feminists need each other – one to sustain their reputation as a wind-up merchant, the other to sustain their feeling of perpetual outrage.

That the authorities would become involved in any part of a woman's private life, let alone the conversations she has, her Twitter account, or the arguments she gets into, is really worrying. Contemporary feminists decry the patriarchy and claim that the system is rigged against women, and yet, in the same breath, they call upon the authorities to meddle in their personal and political lives. The idea that the police would have any interest in specifically protecting women's freedom is laughable – the job of the police isn't to have any serious interest in what is politically best for women. Any woman who values her freedom, and wants to be free to say what she believes, should balk at the idea of state regulation of the internet.

Yes, the internet, and certain social-media platforms in particular, can bring out the worst in some people. Sometimes this is particularly bad. The actress Leslie Jones, who was part of the lead cast for the *Ghostbusters* remake, suffered horrendous abuse online. She was subjected to extremely racist and sexist tweets, on a scale that was genuinely shocking.

But even though this ugly side of the internet, which includes the new alt-right movement, does seem to have a penchant for letting its angst out at female commentators, this shouldn't scare women. By giving in to calls for regulation and censorship, women are letting these spotty keyboard warriors feel like they've won. It's almost like a school-ground battle: the best thing for an annoying bully is to let them know that they don't bother you.

It seems silly having to spell this out, but this is now a controversial viewpoint. On the Everyday Sexism website, one commentator wrote of the importance of having a Safe Space on the internet: 'Because most of the internet is unmoderated, I have only a handful of places on the internet where I know I can be my true self without being disrespected, silenced, or trolled. I need these spaces to remain safe for the sake of my emotional and psychological health.'[22] Feminists are now arguing that it is necessary for women's safety that they don't come into contact with 'disrespectful' comments. What a sad and pathetic downplaying of female power.

The return of the fragile woman

The idea that words are a threat to women is grossly offensive. More dangerous than any tweet or Facebook comment is the idea that women should be protected from language. The cornerstone of a free society is freedom of speech. Without that freedom, all other struggles for liberation are thwarted. Feminists argue that it's only 'hate speech' or 'misogynistic' speech they want to ban, but the definition of these categories expands daily. In the rather brash world of Twitter, many feminists class genuine political criticism of being 'trolling', and view any kind of disagreement

[22] Ferguson, Sian, 'Six Reasons Why We Need Safe Spaces', 5 August 2014, *Everyday Feminism,* (Online)

as a personal attack. How many of us have used the words 'bossy' or 'sweetheart' or 'love'? These words are now considered misogynistic. Everyday language is being policed by the very people who claim to be interested in freedom. By censoring what people can say in the name of women's rights, feminists sacrifice freedom of expression.

Less than 100 years ago, women were considered too fragile and hysterical to deal with the rough and tumble of public life. Politics was too gruff and male for women to engage in, and you weren't supposed to curse or be lewd in front of women, for fear of unbalancing their delicate sensibilities. This ludicrous idea has been revived in the 21st century – only this time, it isn't men calling for the restriction of women's lives, it's feminists.

It is striking that the feminists at the forefront of calls for censorship always talk about safety for *other* women. The media feminists, who make a living from being professionally outraged by supposed online sexism, claim *they* can rise above it – it's the other women out there who can't. And what they really mean by 'other women' is women without a large Twitter following, women who don't have book deals and PHDs – women who are too thick and vulnerable to be able to deal with an insult. It is in their calls for censorship to protect other women that feminists reveal their true prejudice: that working-class, uneducated women need to be protected and looked after, not only by the authorities, but by their smarter, wiser feminist betters.

No one delights in foul and insulting language – as a society committed to freedom and tolerance, we should challenge anyone who oversteps the mark, and argue with ideas we don't like. But calling for bans on language, the tool with which we shape the world around us, is wrong and backward. Moreover, those who stand to lose the most from banning certain words aren't the idiots on Twitter who get their jollies off by calling a woman a slut – it's women themselves. How can any self-respecting, free-thinking woman accept the idea that certain words would make her feel unsafe?

There is a reason why feminism's attitude to free speech is the first point of contention in this book: free speech is the lifeblood of a free society. Feminists' fear of free speech, their desire to censor images and words they don't like, has an impact on wider society. This is not to say that feminism is solely to blame for our current risk-averse, pro-censorship political climate. But in calling for women to be protected and shielded from the throes of public life, feminists are leading a cultural shift – one which removes power from the people to make decisions about their everyday life and hands it to the state. In calling for censorship, feminists are feeding a culture of victimhood, which encourages people to see themselves as reliant on a big-brother-like state to protect them from nasty things.

Very often defences of free speech come with a caveat. This is a feminist speciality. The phrase often goes: 'We believe in free speech but no one has the right to make women feel unsafe.' Free speech must come with no ifs, and no buts. Even if that means getting called a fat slag on Twitter now and then. If that's the price of living in a free society, it's one well worth paying.

2

FEMINISM AND THE BODY

When it comes to language, feminists favour restriction. But when it comes to bodies, contemporary feminists seem to want to let it all hang out. Women's bodies have never been more politicised. Every hair, every spot, every movement is scrutinised and judged. Women can hardly move for being told what they should wear, how they should present themselves in public, even how they should feel about their own body image.

But I'm not talking about the usual scapegoats for making women feel bad – mass advertising or sexist culture. No, today it is feminism that is obsessed with women's bodies.

The Women's March

Do you know what a pussy hat is? It's not a euphemism, it's an actual hat, worn by many of the women who marched in January 2017 to protest against the election of Donald Trump. The Women's March was celebrated as a sign that women weren't going to sit down and take the injustices spouted by Trump. And almost all of the marchers wore 'pussy hats' – hats knitted with ears in a pun on Trump's infamous comment that he grabbed women 'by the pussy'.

These hats are part of a movement, or so the Pussy Hat Project claims:

> *'We chose this loaded word for our project because we want to reclaim the term as a means of empowerment. In this day and age, if we have pussies we are assigned the gender of "woman." Women, whether transgender or cisgender, are mistreated in this society. In order to get fair treatment, the answer is not to deny our femaleness and femininity, the answer is to demand fair treatment. A woman's body is her own. We are honouring this truth and standing up for our rights.* [23]

This could have been seen as just a dig at the president – a bit of fun at a serious protest. But actually, these 'pussy hats' reveal a lot about the general tone of the Women's March. Alongside crude headwear, women carried big hand-drawn signs showing uteruses, vaginas, boobs; they went topless and chanted things that rhymed with pussy, cunt and other nicknames for female genitalia. Women weren't marching against Trump, women's bodies were: the focus of the protests was very much on women's bodies rather than setting out political goals or demanding that Trump stop attacking women's freedom.

If women are to centre their political arguments around their bodies, and fetishise their difference from men by means of brandishing big placards with their genitals scrawled in pink paint, there is no hope of arguing for women's liberation. Women must demand that their arguments for things specific to their body (for example, abortion rights) are won on the grounds of political debate, not by shouting about the bits between their legs.

[23]   *Pussy Hat Project*, 'FAQ'

At the Sydney Women's March, one protester held a sign that simply said 'hands off my bloody pussy', with colour coding for extra impact. This base and crass fetishisation of women's bodies needs further investigation.

The grossness of 'gross-out feminism'

This in-your-face interest in women's bodies might be new, but the obsession with women's biology has been a focus for feminists for years. Just consider some of the books written by feminists in the past 20 years:

The Vagina Monologues by Eve Ensler (1996)

Cunt: A Declaration of Independence by Inga Muscio (1998)

Vagina Warriors by Eve Ensler (2005)

Vagina: A New Biography by Naomi Wolf (2012)

Pussy: A Reclamation by Regena Thomashauer (2016)

Colour Up Next Tuesday (C.U.N.T): A Feminist Colouring Book by Beki Reilly (2016)

So feminists' obsession with women's nether regions has been gathering pace for a few years. It's an easy way of sounding radical to say 'cunt' in a speech or to hold a sign that says 'pussy'. But it doesn't mean anything. The fascination with women's bodies is sheer superficiality. Since the 1980s, feminism has moved from being about liberating women from the kitchen to pushing women back into the bathroom with a mirror in hand, encouraging them to find meaning in staring up their own arseholes.

Behold the latest degradation of women's liberation: gross-out feminism. 'This new movement normalises women by focusing on their bodies, warts and all', Zoe Strimpel writes in the *New Statesman*.[24] 'Its goal is to provide a kind of shock therapy to those still harbouring the notion that women don't have bodily functions, trapped gas, or insubordinate periods.' Lofty ambitions indeed.

'Vaginas are so hot right now. If that sentence shocks you, then you've been out of the cultural loop', she continues. And she's right. Modern feminism *is* obsessed with vaginas. Take the *Guardian*'s new video column, 'Vagina Dispatches', which claims 'there is something particularly damaging about vagina ignorance'.[25] The leaders of the project, two attractive young women, have started up an online hub where readers are invited to draw vulvas and discuss their genitals. They even went out on the streets of New York, one dressed as a vagina, asking people to name the bits.

Remember Charlotte Roche's novel *Wetlands*?[26] The 2008 book which sought to be as disgusting as possible in an attempt to 'normalise' women's bodies? The book about haemorrhoids, anal sex and farting that was hailed as an empowering breakthrough for women's liberation? That piece of fiction has become real. From free-bleeding campaigns to the new fascination with body hair, feminism is now, often literally, staring up its own backside.

The original aim of women's liberation was to fight for a woman's right to leave behind the dishcloths, baby bottles and kitchenware of the private sphere and be as much a part of the public world as any man. Encouraging women to leave the

[24]   Strimpel, Zoe, 'Welcome feminism's new gross-out frontier', 6 October 2016, *New Statesman,* (Online)

[25]   Chalabi, Mona, Ryan, Mae, '10 things you need to know about vaginas', 24 September 2016, *Guardian,* (Online)

[26]   Roche, Charlotte, *Wetlands,* M. DuMont Schauberg, 2008

isolated realm of the private sphere, and thus leave behind their subservient roles as wives and mothers, was what it originally meant to fight for women's rights.

However, following in the footsteps of the women's liberation movement of the early 1970s, an inward-looking feminism emerged, declaring that a woman's private life should be politicised. Lena Dunham, creator of the much-hailed HBO show, Girls, once said 'there's no such thing as too much information'.[27] This is the logical continuation of the old feminist slogan, 'the personal is political'. Rather than insisting women be able to leave the private sphere behind, feminists like Dunham now insist that every private detail of women's lives and bodies be celebrated in public.

Worryingly, this contortion of women's liberation is being embraced by all manner of media feminists. Dunham's love of 'TMI' feminism owes a lot to author and exhibitionist Caitlin Moran, who shared a similar sentiment when she said 'there is no such thing as oversharing' in an interview to promote her semi-autobiographical novel, *How to Build a Girl*[28], in 2014.

But what is a 'real woman' anyway? There is a certain fascination with this idea – adverts are encouraged to feature 'real' women, surveys claim they've talked to 'real' women. Of course, what this actually means is women who aren't models or professional media commentators. The 'real woman' is the feminised 'average Joe'. In fetishising what is 'real', feminists stereotype and demean women. It's no good that you engage women on a political level, you have to relate to them – you have to look and sound and feel 'real'.

Of course, if this gross-out feminism were just a superficial

[27]   i-D staff, 'Lena Dunham to launch young women's newsletter', 14 July 2015, *i-D*, (Online)

[28]   Moran, Caitlin, *How To Build a Girl*, Ebury Press, 2014

interest in leg hair and menstrual cups, most of us would roll our eyes and look the other way. But what this new movement is claiming is that women's bodies should be the focus of feminist politics. Gross-out, TMI feminism drags women back to the state of visceral, biological creatures. This outlook defines women by their bodies, and by nature, not by their ideas or achievements. Fighting the desire to shrug off this creepy obsession with women's privates, in this chapter I will dissect the ways in which contemporary feminists are politicising women's bodies. Let's break it down into feminists' favourite talking points: weight, periods and boobs.

The weight problem

A more recent facet of feminism's obsession with the body has been weight. Fat-shaming, skinny-privilege and body image are now common terms in the feminist dictionary. Ever since fashion changed and skinny models replaced impossibly curvy pin-up girls as the fashionable image, feminists have developed a complex about fat. Women have a problem with their weight, we're told, because society wants us to be thin. Any public comment on weight, or any judgement passed on size or shape, is seen as detrimental to women's mental health.

This extends from music videos to public-health campaigns to adverts – and no advert caught as much flak from feminists as the 2015 UK Protein World campaign. Feminists nationwide spat out their coconut water at the brand's billboard campaign for diet supplements, featuring a bikini-clad Australian model in front of the words: 'Are you beach body ready?'

The feminist commentariat insisted the model, Renee Somerfield, was an unrealistic portrayal of womanhood, and therefore the advert would potentially hurt women's allegedly delicate feelings. 'Not everyone's priority is having a beach body'[29], fumed a Change.org petition, which gained over 50,000 signatures in support of banning the advert from the underground. 'Making somebody feel guilty for not prioritising it by questioning their personal choices is a step too far.'

The feminists who were outraged by this advert essentially took the stereotypical secondary-school girls' toilet conversation about weight and turned it into a political campaign – and with success. London's mayor, Sadiq Khan, banned the adverts from the London underground, stating, 'as the father of two teenage girls, I am extremely concerned about this kind of advertising which can demean people, particularly women, and make them ashamed of their bodies. It is high time it came to an end.'[30]

As with much of what's wrong with contemporary feminism, this obsession with flab and rolls has been gaining ground for the past 30 or 40 years. Almost 40 years ago, *Fat is a Feminist Issue*[31] by Susie Orbach, was published. In it, Orbach argued that weight was not something superficial or cosmetic. Instead, fat is, as *Guardian* journalist Zoe Williams describes it, 'a defence against competition, a way to dance around the painful establishment of hierarchy within your own gender'.[32] Orbach was one of the first feminists to talk about body image and self love in terms of looks. Appearance had been a feminist issue from the 1970s onwards, but it wasn't until *Fat is a Feminist Issue* came out that lardy arses and protruding rib cages became a central focus of feminist discussion.

[29] Baring, Charlotte, 'Remove "Are You Beach Body Ready" Advertisements', Change.org, 2015 (Online)

[30] Crerar, Pippa, 'Sadiq Khan: There will be no more "body shaming" adverts on the Tube', 13 June 2016, *Evening Standard,* (Online)

[31] Orbach, Susie, *Fat is a Feminist Issue: The Anti-diet Guide for Women,* Random House, 1978

[32] Williams, Zoe, 'Susie Orbach: "Not all women used to have eating issues. Now everybody does"', 22 February 2016, *Guardian,* (Online)

When I was a teenager at school, my friends and I used to talk about how we hated campaigns that used the word 'curvy' to make us feel good about ourselves. We thought it was just a nice way of saying fat. There's not a lot you can get past teenage girls. No matter how positively women's bodies are portrayed in the media, they will inevitably worry about the way they look. But this is something that most of us (thankfully) grow out of by the time we leave school.

The backlash against these adverts, and the ban it inspired, treats women like teenage girls. That grown women admitted to feeling intimidated, and even tearful by these images is embarrassing. The overwhelming message from feminists at the time was that images of skinny women made 'normal' women feel worthless. In this way, they were giving ground to the argument that a woman's worth is in her appearance. Rather than saying, 'so what if I'm not beach body ready?', feminists threw a hissy fit.

If we really want to give teenage girls a lasting complex about their appearance, censoring images of women who don't adhere to what is deemed to be 'real' is a good place to start. Restricting women's choices and attempting to shield them from negative images encourages young women to take all of that teenage body-image crap seriously. This is infinitely more damaging than any 10-feet-tall billboard with a skinny Aussie on it. The politicisation of women's body fat, the most apolitical thing imaginable, is detrimental to any argument that attempts to separate a woman's appearance from her worth. Not only is talking about weight boring, it's deeply reactionary.

The period problem

This mildly annoying occurrence, which happens to almost all women, once a month, for much of their lives, is suddenly interesting. Or, at least, feminists seem to find periods interesting. Menstruation is problematised, we're told. Women feel ashamed about their periods, we try to sneak tampons up our sleeves when we need the toilet, and hide stained underwear away from our boyfriends – this is bad. Instead, we should feel proud of our periods, and empowered to free bleed and let the world know that women have periods.

'My name is Lindy West and I'm fat and I bleed out of my hole sometimes. My body is mine now.'[33] This extract from US author and *Guardian* journalist Lindy West's book *Shrill* is an example of just how public feminists want to be with their bodily functions. 'The active ingredient in period stigma is misogyny', West argues. Women who don't discuss their bodily fluid on Twitter or write about it in articles are oppressed, restrained and exhibiting symptoms of internalised misogyny, apparently

This drive to politicise menstruation recently took the form of a campaign to end the tax on tampons in the UK. Tampons are currently taxed along with other items considered to be 'luxury goods'. Feminist campaigners claim this is a 'sexist surcharge'. UK Labour MP Stella Creasy famously shouted 'tampon' at a bumbling Tory MP who was skirting around the issue while discussing the tax until he conceded and used the word 'tampon' in his contribution to the floor. To raise awareness of the campaign against the tampon tax, several women stood outside parliament wearing blood-soaked white jeans.

Obviously sanitary products are not a luxury – they're brilliant inventions which mean that women don't have to spend time washing out rags once a month. So the idea of making tampons and sanitary products cheaper is a good one. But so would an end to the tax on lots of things. In fact, what's so special about tampons? Why are they the one item that should be cheaper? The

---

[33] West, Lindy, 'Break the period taboo: my name is Lindy West and I bleed', 9 May 2016, *Guardian*, (Online)

feminist focus on this one minuscule area of a woman's life shows its obsession with trivial issues. It's salacious to bleed in your white jeans outside Westminster. It's controversial to talk about the p-word in political debate. It's a feminist trump card – you can't possibly understand periods unless you've had one.

This has damaging consequences. In March 2016, a British organisation called Co-Exist wanted to set up a 'period policy' in the workplace, which would allow women time off for their time of the month.[34] This was celebrated by feminists as a way to make the workplace more equal and safe for women. This bizarre idea cements the truly sexist notion that women are beholden to their bodies – that their freedom and capability to act in the world is dependent on their menstruation cycle.

This is a deeply backward idea. Teenage girls moan about how awful it is to have to deal with all that comes with periods – women understand that these conversations are enormously boring. It's like discussing how inconvenient it is that once a day every human being has to take a dump. If we want to have a conversation about how to revolutionise birth control so that women can control their periods and fertility more effectively and easily, let's. But the period panic wants nothing to do with innovation or practicality; instead it is content with specialising periods as some kind of oppression against women. The fact is, periods are life, they're trivial, and talking about them on *Newsnight* is certainly not furthering women's freedom.

The battle over breasts

If you want to be a good feminist today, it seems you must also have an opinion on breasts.

And you would expect the two main sides in the contemporary

---

[34] Ridley, Louise, 'UK Company Coexist Is Launching A "Period Policy" And It's Not Shy About Telling Everyone', 2 March 2016, *Huffington Post*, (Online)

feminist bra debate – the campaign to Free the Nipple and the (now defunct) No More Page 3 campaign – to be in permanent conflict. One is about exposing nipples, the other about covering them up.

But, as a piece in the *Huffington Post* put it, '#FreetheNipple and No More Page 3 share the same feminist goal: greater equality for women'.[35] But how can feminists want to bin their bras and strap them back on with moral zeal at the same time?

This paradox seems to be making a statement about the purpose of breasts. It suggests that, sometimes, it's okay for boobs to be on display – other times it isn't. Another article argued that 'nobody can surely say they open Page 3 to see what nature has created to feed children?'.[36] The implication here seems to be that when breasts are a source of food for babies, they're good; but when they are displayed in a more sexual way, they're bad.

This depiction of boobs as simply udders is completely regressive. Like feminists' obsession with other parts of the body, it sets back women's equality by prioritising the biology of the female over her autonomy as a free-thinking individual able to decide what she likes and what she doesn't like. What about women who don't have kids? What about women who can't breastfeed? What about women who simply don't want to breastfeed and prefer to celebrate the playfulness of breasts over their instrumental use?

What constitutes a good, wholesome, feminist pair of tits? It seems that showing them to other good, wholesome feminists is a good start. The specification of where and when women should be allowed to bare all – on Instagram, yes; in the *Sun*, no – is really

[35] Dale, Elisabeth, '#FreetheNipple and NoMorePage3: Changing Our View of Women's Breasts', 7 October 2014, *Huffington Post*, (Online)

[36] Booth, Samantha, 'Free the Nipple vs Page Three', 4 February 2015, *Huffington Post*, (Online)

about censoring who is allowed to look at breasts. For feminists, it is okay for like-minded females, babies and men who have pledged their support via Twitter to see breasts, but gruff builders, young lads and pretty much anyone who finds tits titillating can't be allowed to glimpse a freed nipple.

This is what I like to call The Good, The Bad and The Ugly of boobs. Good, clever, petite middle-class breasts are acceptable; bad, fake, bulging Essex-girl breasts are not. And The Ugly? Well, that would have to be the array of obsequious male nipples appearing under the #FreetheNipple hashtag on social-media platforms like Instagram.

Feminists who support both #FreetheNipple and No More Page 3 reveal themselves to be not only embarrassed by their fellow females who choose to get their knockers out for cash rather than retweets, but also openly prejudiced about a working-class girl's ability to make her own decisions about her body. So the likes of former glamour model and reality TV star Katie Price are seen as a dangerous influence on women because they aren't puritanical about their chests. Feminists find this extremely threatening. In her book *How To Be A Woman*, Caitlin Moran described Price as 'Vichy France with tits'[37]. Alas, what Moran and her political colleagues fail to understand is that in demeaning and undermining what they deem to be 'bad' women, it is they who are collaborating with the enemy. In positing a strict idea of what women's bodies should be used for, and in demonising (as Moran does in her how-to guide on feminism) the lifestyles of working-class young women, they align themselves with the same kind of snobbery and elitism they claim to rail against.

Last year, UK Labour MP Harriet Harman defended reality TV star Kim Kardashian's naked selfies, claiming 'there's a kind

[37]   Moran, Caitlin, *How To Be A Woman*, Ebury Press, 2011, Pg 252

of bravery and pioneering spirit in them'.[38] But, when asked if she felt the same way about topless girls on Page 3, Harman did not apply the same praise. 'The Kardashian girls are controlling their own agenda. The thing about the Page 3 girls in the *Sun* [who, in fact, no longer appear in the paper] is that the male editors are producing these young girls for the male readers.' So much for fighting for independence, even the independence to sell pictures of your boobs. Harman and other feminists are clearly stating a difference between rich, cool, Kardashian boobs and working-class, Page 3 boobs. Today's middle-class feminists are really only interested in enforcing a top-down puritanism about nudity and control of working-class behaviour.

What this boob-obsessed bunch can't face up to is that no one outside of their tiny cliques really cares about what happens to our chests. The world of Page 3 is old-fashioned, yes, but hardly worth getting your bra strap in a twist over. Scour Instagram, and you will see the hypocrisy of #FreetheNipple: this hashtag campaign contains promiscuous selfies and shots of casually pierced nipples, all accompanied by token lines about the need to be nice to women. These breast barers are just as keen for attention as those who pose for tabloids, which is all well and good, but they think they're involved in a moral cause because their 'likes' come from middle-class professional Instagrammers rather than oiks in a greasy-spoon cafe.

If we believe that women have the right to do whatever the hell they want with their bodies, then for God's sake can we talk about something other than tits? Young middle-class feminists see it as their duty to educate stupid men and stupid women about the parameters of breast-baring, about acceptable and unacceptable boobs. But women have a far better tool, above the chest – can we please engage that instead?

[38] Harman, Harriet, 24 May 2016, *Good Morning Britain*, ITV (TV)

The case for real bodily autonomy

Please, let's forget about periods, boobs, fat rolls and body hair. These things don't matter. In fact, the obsession with appearance is taking energy and attention away from the very real threat to women's bodily autonomy that is still prevalent in the 21st Century: abortion rights.

In the UK, abortion is not free and legal − a woman has to seek permission from two doctors, and prove a pregnancy would mentally harm her, before she is allowed access to an abortion. In Northern Ireland, abortion is still illegal under the 1861 Offences Against the Person Act, as the 1967 Abortion Act, which partially decriminalised abortion in England, Scotland and Wales, does not apply there. Women who are found guilty of having an abortion face a sentence of up to life in prison. In the Republic of Ireland, abortion is also illegal, under the much-protested Eighth Amendment to the Irish Constitution.

The story is no better across the pond. In the US, *Roe v Wade* makes abortion technically legal, but different states have different restrictions on abortion (some call it feticide) which make it very difficult for women to access medical services. At the time of writing, in Texas, governors are attempting to pass a bill which would require women to cover the funeral costs of an aborted fetus, an obvious discrimination against poor women who can barely afford the expense of an abortion in the first place. The state of Arkansas has just passed a law which allows a woman's rapist to sue in order to prevent abortion. And it's only in the Western area of Australia that abortion is available legally on request, and even then it's still only available up to 20 weeks.

Women are in desperate need of a movement that demands

their right to bodily autonomy. But abortion is one of those areas that feminists don't seem too keen to touch. The answer is simple: the only way to ensure women's freedom over their own bodies is to remove abortion and all other reproductive services from criminal law.

This means that any woman can have an abortion at any time during her pregnancy for any reason. Anything less than that, including limits on timing or condition, insinuates that there are points at which women can't be trusted to make the final decision about their pregnancy. If we believe women know best what is right for their bodies, then we must argue for requesting an abortion to be as quick and simple as asking for any other medical procedure. In this way, women are realised and supported by society as autonomous, trusted, equal individuals.

This same principle applies to prostitution. Many feminists support the model of prohibition which criminalises men who use prostitutes but safeguards the women engaged in said prostitution. The problem in this approach is, again, that women are not trusted to make their own decisions. If we truly believe in women's freedom, we must support a woman's right to use her body in any way she sees fit. If that means risking the danger of standing out on a street corner, so be it. We must treat women like the independent, capable adults they are. Women must be free not only to make their own decisions but to deal with the consequences of those decisions.

The narcissus

The birth of third-wave feminism in the 1980s and 1990s revealed a shift in focus for feminists. No longer were they arguing against women being cooped up in the home, separated from public life and treated differently to men, instead they turned their attention to how best to shape public life so that it mirrored the private sphere, and felt 'safer' and 'nicer' for women. Anti-porn feminists argued that the outside world had to be made safe and inoffensive for women, just as if they were cosy at home. The same argument is now made in terms of women's image of themselves – a woman's self esteem must be protected, her image continuously congratulated and praised by society."

In this way, late feminism has largely contributed to the shrinking of the public sphere. No longer does feminism look to what women can contribute and gain from engagement in public life; instead its goal is to make public life more personal and emotional to suit what feminists see as women's inherent nature. When feminists tell people that no one can understand what it's like to be a woman if you haven't had a period or put on weight around your thighs or been called an ugly bitch on Twitter, what they're essentially arguing is that women's being is tied up in their physicality. Women are inextricably linked to their biology – their menstruation, their weight, their genitals – and this influences their political capabilities. Women can't hear criticism of their weight because their weight is intrinsic to their sense of self. Women shouldn't be discreet about their periods because periods are integral to their rational capabilities. Women shouldn't bare their breasts because that is to give in to their oppression. For a movement so supposedly liberated, contemporary feminism seems to sound more and more like a Victorian manual.

As with other areas of feminists' attacks on women's freedom, this obsession with the body has a nasty anti-working class undertone to it. This was beautifully displayed by one of my favourite UK shows: *The Only Way is Essex (TOWIE). TOWIE* is a reality TV show which follows young men and women around at home in Essex, the home of cockneys. The girls featured in the show indulge in beauty treatments and go out and get so drunk they don't remember who they kissed – great TV. But one famous scene made UK feminists very angry – when one character got 'vajazzled'. Vajazzling is essentially be-jewelling, trimming and generally giving a woman's pubic area a makeover. A great laugh, right? Wrong.

In a scathing article against cosmetic surgery, UK feminist Bridget Christie slammed beauty trends and body augmentation: 'I'm a mum now. My body doesn't need to be perfect, it just needs to work. As long as I can pick up my children, throw them into a bin and run away really quickly, that's all that matters. And I can't do that with enormous mattress-filled breasts, bound feet or convalescing labia.'[39] Middle-class feminists' scorn for women who want to look a certain way or spend time on their appearance is palpable. The girls on *TOWIE* are the incarnate of everything they hate – dressing up for male attention.

I much prefer the *TOWIE* narcissism to the self-obsession inherent in feminists' drive to politicise women's bodies. Never mind about some guy telling you your leg hair is a bit long, or feeling a little bit bad about your skinny co-worker, or hiding tampons up your sleeve on the way to the loo. The real battle for women's bodies starts and ends with freedom. And this battle is much bigger, and far more profound than contemporary feminists with their shallow and vain campaigns seem to understand. Rather than embarking on yet more awareness-raising schemes about hollow preoccupations with women's bodies, let's get to grips with what could really make women free. Let's get serious about bodily autonomy.

---

[39] Christie, Bridget, 'Bridget Christie on body image: "We're slicing ourselves up like a Solihull Toby Carvery on pension day"' 23 June 2015, *Guardian,* (Online)

3

FEMINISM AND SEX

Never before has sex been more problematic. Not even in Victorian times, when women were shamed for showing a bit of ankle, was there such a furore over women's sex lives. Today, it's not prudish censors who are panicking about what women get up to; rather, it is feminists who are stunting women's sexual freedom.

Moral panics are often phrased in terms of 'cultures'. Gang culture, or drug culture, for example. The latest trend among the perpetually panicked is rape culture. Rape culture, as feminists describe it, is the idea that we are living in a society which either glorifies or allows behaviour that is deemed 'rapey'. It's not the case that there has been an increase in rape, or that women are suffering from physical abuse more frequently. Instead, rape is redefined, not as a violent act, but as something which can describe a variety of behaviours.

In this way, the normal, messy play of sexual relations is being problematised. Feminists encourage women to see every sexual encounter not as a potentially exciting experience, but as something risky and dangerous. Women are encouraged to see sex as something during which they must have their guard up. Sex for women must always be restricted, controlled and navigated through norms and rules. For men, sex is something which they have to learn to do right – men must be trained to *not* rape women, and force back their supposed natural instincts to abuse women.

The myth of rape culture

In order to explain this relatively frightening idea of a 'rape culture', and to understand how so many women have decided to buy in to this problematic framing of sexual relations, let's look at where feminists say rape culture is most pronounced – on university campuses.

Back in 2010, the UK National Union of Students released a report called 'Hidden Marks: A study of women students' experiences of harassment, stalking, violence and sexual assault'.[40] The report asked 2,058 participants about their experiences on campus. It claimed that '14 per cent [of women] have experienced serious physical or sexual assault. 68 per cent have been subject to verbal or physical sexual harassment', and 'nearly one in four has experienced unwanted sexual contact'. The problem with this report is that it lays out serious physical assault, verbal harassment and unwanted sexual conduct on a scale. It isn't even clear if the physical assault was classified as rape, instead, 'unwanted sexual conduct' is used as the base line of negative experience, and every other classification is on a sliding scale up from that point.

This is crucial, because, when digging in to the report's research, it quickly becomes apparent that the stats don't stand up. The report deliberately mystifies the topic under discussion. It says, 'violence

---

against women can be defined in a number of different ways'[41], which is curious – wouldn't most people define violence against women as someone being violent towards a woman? Not according to *Hidden Marks*, which defines it as: 'Generally understood as gendered violence experienced by women, which can include physical, sexual, emotional, psychological and financial abuse, as well as threatening, coercive and controlling behaviour.' Violence is here redefined – it's not just hurting someone physically, it's being mean to them, or nicking their money, or persuading them to do something for you. When defining sexual harassment, the report is even more vague: 'There is no strict definition of the term sexual harassment, but it is commonly understood to describe unwelcome behaviour of a sexual nature.'

Arguably this definition could apply as much to a bad chat-up line or a wink across the bar as it could to rape or serious sexual assault. This blurring of distinctions is really bad for women, because if sexual harassment can mean something really not that serious at all (like a wolf whistle) then how are women to be taken seriously when something serious happens? By redefining sexual assault as something less specific than what it is – a serious physical attack on a woman of a sexual nature that isn't rape – feminists are undermining the severity of what it really means. If sexual harassment is everywhere at all times, then it's nowhere and means nothing.

Hidden Marks continuously contradicts itself. It begins by stating that one in seven women have been sexually assaulted on campus. This shocking stat would make you think that most women would not want to return to their campus grounds – or would at least feel uneasy about their safety there. But no, the report later states: 'Nearly all respondents who visited their

[41]   *Hidden Marks,* Pg 8

university or college buildings during the day always, or mostly, felt safe.'[42] Why would a woman feel safe at a place where she was likely to be sexually assaulted – even in the daytime? The questions participants were asked were engineered to produce the most extreme results possible – in a question about sexual harassment, the examples included things like being quizzed about your love life.

But most importantly, the report admits that it began with bias. 'We were particularly interested in students' experiences of sexual violence, given the recent publication of a number of opinion polls about attitudes to rape victims'[43], it reads. *Hidden Marks* is a piece of advocacy research, with the intended aim of finding cause to panic about women's sexual experiences on campus. The sample of participants were self-selecting, meaning student-activist types who shared the survey's perspective on gendered violence presumably made up most of the selection. If you have someone who describes 'unwanted kissing' as sexual violence answering a survey about rape culture on campus, it's not surprising that the results will be rather shocking.

Despite the huge flaws and inaccuracies in this report, it has come to define much of feminists' work on campus. Feminist meetings are no longer about fighting for women's freedom, they're now interested in prohibiting women's independence on campus. A large number of universities and students' unions in the UK now hold policies such as 'Zero Tolerance to Harassment', which, based on the findings of reports like *Hidden Marks,* threaten to discipline students who are seen to be in breach of sexual-behaviour codes. This means that when some unfortunate lad tries his luck at the bar, as many do in the

---

[42]   *Hidden Marks,* Pg 9
[43]   Ibid, Pg 17

messy play of the first encounters of a relationship, and leans in a little too close to deliver his pick-up line, he could in theory be reported for harassment.

Not only does this approach completely undermine what serious sexual assault is, and to a great extent trivialise rape, it also invites an external authority into the private sexual lives of adults. Of course *Hidden Marks* is not solely to blame for feminism's warped take on women's sexual freedom, but it has been the springboard for many reforms and restrictions enacted on campuses in the UK. The discussion of 'rape culture' has influenced feminists on campus worldwide – picking up where anti-porn and conservative feminists left off in the 1990s.

The rape-culture panic has turned back the clock for female students. In the 1960s, when women were literally put under curfew to protect them from the imaginary dangers of the opposite sex, feminists fought against the nannying and overbearing protection of the university. As the freedom-fighting feminist Camille Paglia famously put it, women fought for the freedom 'to risk rape'. This didn't mean that women were supposed to smile and accept unwanted sexual contact from men, whether it be negligible or criminal, but it meant that women were as free as men to deal with their sexual encounters as they saw fit. No university administration laying out rules for their conduct, no students' unions penalising fellow students for inappropriate flirting.

This has all changed. Women are now encouraged to see university as acting *in loco parentis*. Students' unions in the UK act more like parents than unions, regulating students' behaviour in their private lives in order to protect women from dangerous encounters. This deeply reactionary move is framed in terms of looking after women, or exhibiting 'decent' behaviour. But all it really does is invite external judgement into women's private lives, and feed the idea that women are vulnerable creatures in need of protection from public life.

The Mattress Girl

And who suffers most from these developments on campus? Women. Female students are now starting to believe that university is a dangerous place for them to be. Women are beginning to redefine their sexual experiences as sexual assault, where they previously didn't view their encounters as untoward. Not only this, but women are also encouraged to wear their negative experiences around their necks as part of their identity. There is something very troubling about feminists' desire to publicise sexual assault.

Of course, it's not that feminists want sexual assaults to continue to happen, but their morbid fetishisation of women's negative sexual encounters is highly problematic. There are actual Twitter campaigns which encourage women to indulge in every negative incident they face by tweeting about it. Hollaback, a website which started up in New York but now has sister organisations worldwide, is solely focused on documenting women's negative experiences. But the vast majority of these are nothing serious – 'this guy looked sideways at me on the tube', or 'this man told me I looked attractive'. All of this feeds into contemporary feminists' narrative that women suffer daily sexual abuse – and it's just not true.

This strange fascination with sexual assault was best captured in 2014 on Columbia University campus in New York, when a young woman called Emma Sulkowicz decided to turn her alleged rape into an art project.

In 2013, Sulkowicz accused fellow student Paul Nungesser of rape, filing a criminal complaint to the NYPD and campus authorities eight months after the incident. Both claims were dismissed, but Sulkowicz wanted to force Nungesser off campus. This idea turned into her senior art thesis in 2014, titled 'Mattress Performance (Carry That Weight)', a performance art piece which involved Sulkowicz carrying a mattress with her whenever she was on campus.

The idea behind the project was to 'get my rapist off campus'[44], as Sulkowicz put it in a interview with the college paper. But her performance took on a new meaning when it was inevitably picked up by the international press. The mattress soon became a symbol of the movement to reform campus sexual-assault proceedings, with feminists worldwide praising Sulkowicz as brave and pioneering.

Talking to Jessica Valenti, a feminist and journalist based in the US, Sulkovicz said of Mattress Performance: 'It's going to be an endurance piece. In some ways, battling rape always has been.'[45] Valenti wrote that Sulkowicz's comment was one 'most people who care about the issue of violence against women can relate to'.

But it's actually worth unpicking this notion of endurance. Assuming that someone *has* gone through a negative sexual experience, that person's reaction to that experience will always be subjective. The emotions involved in getting hurt are outside of the political realm, and quite obviously vary with context. So the idea that rape is something that women have to continuously battle with, and carry around with them like a mattress on their

---

[44] Grasdalen, Taylor, 'Speaking With Emma Sulkowicz', 5 September 2014, *BWOG,*

[45] Valenti, Jessica, 'Beyond "no means no": the future of campus rape prevention is "yes means yes"', 2 September 2014, *Guardian,* (Online)

back, is also a subjective interpretation of a personal experience. Many women who have been raped go on to live full, healthy and carefree lives. The crime they suffered was no less terrible, they just dealt with the aftermath in a different way. In fact, encouraging women to carry their rape like a mattress on their back is a hugely problematic and negative reaction to such a terrible event. The idea that a woman should have to carry the weight of rape, a terrible experience that she never asked for, is completely unjust.

The feminist support for Sulkowicz claimed she was engaging in a selfless act on behalf of all women who couldn't speak up, and was giving a voice to the women who in the future would have the same thing happen to them. But actually, all that the Mattress Performance did was cement the idea that rape changes women. It's almost like a scarlet letter – once a woman has been raped or sexually abused, she's tainted. By painting women as forever tortured by such experiences and unable to escape from a history which they did not choose, feminists are undermining the chance for women to claim back what they lost during their assault – their freedom. The freedom to not be a woman who was assaulted or raped. It goes without saying that any half-decent person will realise the magnitude of a crime like rape, and sympathy, support and justice should be given to the victim. But to fetishise rape as part of a woman's identity is to insult her freedom by seeking to define her as something completely external to her sense of self. In this way, justice is actually thwarted – the woman is still unable to escape her assailant.

In fetishising a woman's rape or sexual assault, feminists inextricably link women with the experiences in their lives over which they had least control. Sulkowicz was completely comfortable with being identified as a rape victim. Of course, there is nothing wrong with being a rape victim. But the problem is, by making this terrible and undesired moment in a woman's life a part of her identity, she then wears the label 'victim'. In this sense, a woman's active agency is chipped away; she is no longer someone who defines herself, but is defined by this act that was forced upon her. Instead of encouraging women to leave aside (as best they can) this act that was never part of their intended identity, feminists encourage women to engrain a sense of victimhood into the core of their being.

What a terrible injustice this is. Not only do rape victims lose control over the moments in which the brutal act is committed, they then must carry the weight of this act with them, rather than put it behind them and move on with their life. This politicisation and fetishisation of victimhood only serves to prolong the horror felt by a rape victim.

The meaning of Yes means Yes

Campus art projects aside, the narrative around rape culture on campus, and the idea that women are at threat from violence during their university lives, has had damaging consequences. The panic over women's sexual experiences has inevitably led to a backlash against sexual freedom. No longer are feminists willing to campaign for the idea that women must be free – even if that means free to risk rape. Instead, they're pushing for new laws and regulation on campus to enable the authorities to limit women's sexual freedom in the name of protecting them from harm.

This takes its most pertinent form in affirmative consent law, or 'yes means yes' consent. This suggested change to rape law would mean that participants in sexual activity have to legally obtain affirmative consent (someone saying, 'Yes, I want to do this) in order to make sure that the following sexual activity is not rape. This technically means that any risky, surprising, romantic gestures are to be reclassified as non-consensual sexual conduct. What happens to spur-of-the-moment romance? When Richard Gere swept Debra Winger into his arms in that hat, he didn't get affirmative consent. When Ryan Gosling pulled Rachel McAdams in for a kiss in the pouring rain, he didn't ask her for permission. The idea of affirmative consent effectively kills romance – it says that all sexual encounters must be preempted. Intrigue, impulse and sexual drive are unsafe and must be locked away.

What's at stake in this policing of sexual encounters isn't actually the prevention of rape. Rape happens in spite of consent. It doesn't actually matter whether someone says yes or no. No, consent classes and reform of consent in the law are all about restricting, policing and problematising normal, private sexual encounters between adults. Instead, it's got everything to do with restricting, policing and problematising normal, private sexual encounters between adults.

Of course, stating 'yes' formally before any action is not how normal relationships operate. Most people who end up in sexual encounters do so because both parties want to be in that scenario. One person takes a risk and leans in for a kiss – this is how the best relationships start, with a spark. But feminists don't seem to agree. A 2015 *Guardian* article written by law professor Jay Sterling Silver states that 'the only people who need to fear an affirmative consent standard for rape are rapists'.[46] What this means, is that if you oppose the idea of relationships needing to begin with official, formal and verbal consent, you're either a rapist or a rape apologist. People who like spontaneity are perverse, and it's only those who can restrain their sexual feelings, and formalise them, that have good intentions.

---

[46]   Sterling Silver, Jay, 'The only people who need to fear an affirmative consent standard for rape are rapists', 20 February 2015, *Guardian*, (Online)

This may seem like a nightmarish re-working of a Mary Whitehouse-style rule book on proper sexual conduct. But in the wake of the uproar following Sulkovicz's performance in the US, this restrained and reactionary view of human sexuality has been given ground. A California bill, passed in 2014, introduced an 'affirmative consent standard' in the determinating of whether consent was given in alleged rape cases. This means that, legally, someone who has not acquired affirmative consent – that is, got the other person to say, 'Yes, I'm into this', out loud, before any action – is potentially a rapist.

This is shocking. In the name of protecting women from rape, feminists are supporting further state and legal intervention into women's private sexual lives. Not only does this problematise sex, feeding the idea that it is a danger to be navigated rather than a pleasure to be explored – it also positions women as the eternal victim. If a man has to verbally acquire consent before he makes a move, this insinuates that the woman should not trust him not to be a rapist. If one has to ask for consent in a situation in which consent is clearly implied, surely that brings doubt into an otherwise trusting situation. A similar thing now happens at doctors' surgeries in England, where female patients will be asked if they'd like a chaperone if they have to remove items of clothing. This means that in an otherwise trusting scenario – the patient trusts that the doctor is there to help rather than abuse – an element of doubt is introduced. If women believed that doctors were going to attack them without a chaperone, why would they feel more comfortable with a chaperone? The same applies for affirmative consent. Why would a man have to ask if you trust that he's not going to rape you?

With terrible exceptions aside (and they are exceptions – we must remind ourselves that the majority of men are not out to hurt or rape women), the fact is that most sexual encounters are fine and it is damaging always to suspect that they won't be. Are women expected to enter into all relationships with that element of doubt, with the fear that unless they classify exactly what they do and don't like verbally before entering into a physical encounter, they will be harmed? The idea that men come to sexual encounters with no idea of when a woman isn't reciprocating is nonsense. Are feminists really willing to sign up to the idea that young men can't tell the difference between someone who is reciprocating sexual intentions and a passed-out girl, or someone explicitly telling them to stop? Do we really believe we have a young generation of rapists in waiting?

This is not a new fear – the underlying message of anti-porn feminism in the 1980s was that men were dangerous and had to be curtailed. The inheritors of the anti-porn movement, feminists like Julie Bindel, claim that men are inherently predetermined to rape women – simply because we live in a sexist culture. Other feminists are more nuanced, but in their support for protective legislation around sex, they show that they share the same sentiment.

In *Defending Pornography,* Nadine Strossen reveals what impact this view of men, as 'rapacious beasts' really has. In changing the law in the name of preventing men from raping – either by banning pornography or introducing laws which create the necessity for formal consent – feminists are removing men's agency. It's not that this man decided he was going to rape this women, he only did it because it's in his nature – he's a victim of a patriarchal and misogynistic society. How would he know any better? Strossen explains it well:

> *'Those who are committed to assisting victims of misogynistic violence – rather than to treating their assailants as victims of*

pornography – and those who are committed to addressing the root causes of such violence, advocate constructive alternative measures not the continued demonisation of pornography.' [47]

Changing the law to require affirmative consent, or banning the kind of 'triggers' that feminists think make men more 'rapey', will do nothing to deter rapists. This is not a deterrent to rape, but merely a crude attempt to further police men's and women's sexual lives. That feminists can't see how pointless and harmful this suggestion is for women's freedom is the true tragedy.

The real problem with sexual freedom

Overblown stats and fabricated panics about a mythical 'rape culture' have spread from the campus bubble of nuts student politics and are now an ever-present feature of feminists' discussions of women's daily experiences. An article in the *Independent* listed '22 signs we live in a rape culture'.[48] These included the fact that women's bodies are objectified on television and that women are supposedly targeted by online gendered abuse. So rape culture actually has nothing to do with rape at all – it simply means anything negative that is directed at women. Cat-calling is rape culture; jokes in poor taste are rape culture; adverts showing women in bikinis are rape culture.

What this simultaneously achieves is a denigration of the seriousness of rape and a ridiculing of the serious fight for women's sexual freedom. Panics about sexual assault become mundane – if you're always potentially at threat, but that threat never materialises, then the threat becomes watered down. Feminists are hampering a serious conversation about women's freedom with hysteria over

---

[47] *Defending Pornography,* Page 274

[48] indy100 staff, '22 signs we live in a rape culture', 7 June 2016, *Independent,* (Online)

minor incidents. Calling a guy at the bar who has danced a little too close 'rapey' is a misunderstanding of the serious nature of rape. It's insulting and wrong.

One rape is one rape too many. It's still the case that most women will feel uncomfortable catching late-night transport alone. If I bump into a man on my own late at night on a dark street, my heart will still race a little faster than if I had walked past a woman with a baby that I'd come across. This is something that, as a society that believes in freedom, we still have to work out. It's unacceptable for anyone to feel at risk from any kind of violent act. That rape cases still happen, in all sorts of scenarios, means that the argument for women's sexual freedom must still be made. But this is not evidence that we still live in a sexist and dangerous world. In the West, women are far safer than ever before – especially on university campuses. Through struggles for freedom, women have won the right to walk home in tiny skirts without shame or harassment. We've changed what was once a truly sexist culture. Claims that women can't walk home without being harassed on a Friday night are plainly untrue.

More than ever, women have to make the case that their sexual lives be free from state intervention, free from legal restraint and free from outside judgement. When a woman needs help from the authorities, the service of justice should be swift and efficient. But in order to combat any lingering fear of dark alleys and lone night-bus rides, women cannot succumb to being painted as potential victims. If we are to enjoy sexual freedom, we must demand it. That means fighting back against any guy who puts his hand down your trousers after you've told him to leave you alone. That means reporting rape immediately, without shame, and with the support and solidarity of other individuals. That means taking your sexual encounters into your own hands, and encouraging women to be strong contenders – not deferring to the law or campus authorities to figure out how to interpret your own feelings. If a man does something we don't like, our first port of call shouldn't be to go crying to the authorities to sort it out. We should encourage women, especially young women, to feel that they can handle situations themselves. When things get too difficult to handle – as unfortunately they sometimes do – that's when the state should be called upon to help us. Outside of that, women should throw off the shackles feminists and the authorities are attempting to close around our ankles and our bedposts.

Beyond what this all means for women, this move to preemptively police sexual encounters has opened up a can of worms in relation to presumed innocence. There have been several online feminist campaigns which use the hashtag #BelieveTheVictim, raising awareness about how the law supposedly does not believe women who are victims of rape.

This is a short-sighted and dangerous view. What happens to innocent until proven guilty if there is a culture which is encouraging the law to believe the accuser? What if someone is lying – as happened in the recent case of over 50 refugees from the Middle East, who were accused of sexually assaulting dozens of women in Frankfurt on New Year's Eve 2016? These accusations, which made international headlines and fuelled racist stereotyping of dangerous Arab men, as well as feeding a panic around immigration, were a hoax.

Feminists are literally changing the law, and it's extremely worrying. In calling for the suspension of the presumption of innocence, feminists put our liberty in jeopardy and render us all increasingly powerless before a state which decides what is the truth on the basis of feelings, rather than evidence. This relationship between feminists and the state, which began in earnest back in the 1980s, has led to this: women being expected to ask for formal and legal consent before they engage in private personal relationships.

The state and the police should always be a woman's last option. Before that, we must cultivate a sense that sexual freedom is won through demand – a demand that women be free to engage in whatever behaviour they choose. Scaring women off sex, and painting sex as a battlefield, will never win us the argument for true sexual freedom.

4

FEMINISM AT WORK

It's illegal to discriminate against employees on the basis of their sex. If an employer is seen to be treating a female employee unfairly, simply because of her gender, the he can be taken to court. In this way, by law, women are equal to men in the workplace.

Believe it or not, this is a controversial statement to make. Feminists argue that, despite women's equality under the law, there is a culture in workplace environments that discriminates against women. Feminists argue that women are held back from aspiring to top jobs, that women find it harder to have successful, high-paid careers, and that women are disadvantaged by sexist behaviour at work.

There are three central myths peddled by contemporary feminism: that women are conditioned into thinking they're not good enough for jobs, that the gender pay gap stops women from achieving, and that the workplace is still dominated by typically male behaviour. Let's be clear from the start: none of these claims are true.

There are obstacles that still stand in the way of women achieving their full potential in the workplace, but these are infinitely more complex than the idea of the glass ceiling is yet to be smashed. That ceiling was smashed years ago, but feminists are still willing to cut themselves on the shards for the sake of being seen to bleed.

The myth of the gender pay gap

Let's begin with feminism's most coveted myth: the gender pay gap. In March 2015, on International Women's Day, the UN reported it would take 70 years for the gender pay gap to close.[49] In November 2015, the World Economic Forum released a report which claimed that it would take 118 years for the gender pay gap to close.[50] In November 2016, the *Guardian* reported on a study conducted by the UK Fawcett Society, which claimed that the gap would take 60 years to close.[51] The Fawcett study also claimed that, due to the pay gap, women would effectively be working for free for the remainder of that year.

So, what exactly is the pay gap for women in the UK? Every week there seem to be new stats out about how disadvantaged women are at work. Will it be 70 years, 118 years or 60 years until we're free from the grip of sexist employers?

The truth is, almost all stats used by gender pay gap enthusiasts are based on average pay. This means that hours, job role and experience are not taken into account. Reports on the gender pay gap compare part-time work with full-time, managerial roles, with beginner roles and long-term employee salaries with newly employed salaries.

[49]   Topping, Alexandra, 'Gender pay gap will not close for 70 years at current rate, says UN', 5 March 2015, *Guardian,* (Online)

[50]   Grimley, Naomi, 'Gender pay gap 'may take 118 years to close' – World Economic Forum' 19 November 2015, BBC, (Online)

[51]   Press Association, 'Gender pay gap means women "working for free from now until 2017"', 10 November 2016, *Guardian,* (Online)

When comparing like for like work, based on the same hours and the same skill level, there is no gender pay gap. In fact, in the UK, young women are earning more than men. According to data from 2015, produced by the Office for National Statistics (ONS), 'between the ages of 22 and 29, a woman will typically earn £1,111 more per annum than her male counterparts'.[52] Earlier this year, the ONS released further statistics, reporting that 'the gender pay gap has fallen from an average of 16 percent for baby-boomers born between 1946 and 1965, to 9 per cent for Generation X, born between 1966 and 1980, and to 5 percent for millennials, or those born between 1981 and 2000'.[53] According to these stats, the pay gap is all but disappearing. In 2016, then minister for the UK Women and Equalities committee, Nicky Morgan, said: 'We've virtually eliminated the gap for full-time workers under 40 and the gap for the over-40s is shrinking too.'[54]

When you think about it, the idea that employers would pay women lower wages for the same work makes no sense. If bosses could get away with paying women less, why would they hire men? And, more to the point, if discrimination against women is so widespread, and believed to be happening so frequently, why aren't feminists taking to the streets about it?

The pay gap is a myth – and most feminists know it. Waxing lyrical about the pay gap is a way for politicians and public figures to prove their feminist credentials. Being angry about the pay gap is the political equivalent of wearing a 'this is what a feminist looks like' t-shirt – it means nothing. The pay gap panic is creating a scandal out of thin air. If women believe that they're walking

[52] Press Association, 'Women in their 20s earn more than men of same age, study finds', 29 August 2015, *Guardian*, (Online)

[53] Carvalho, Ritvik, 'Gender pay gap halves for millennials, but will widen with age: study' 4 January 2017, *Reuters*, (Online)

[54] Williams, Joanna, 'The gender pay gap is dead', 15 February 2016, *spiked*, (Online)

into the job market at a disadvantage, it's more than likely that they will lower their aspirations. Instead of encouraging equality, fearmongering about the pay gap increases the chances that women won't go for top positions.

This doesn't mean that there isn't room for improvement. The only area in which women suffer pay differences for the same job is after they have children. Of course, having children means sacrificing lots of things, not least your ability to hold down a tough, high-flying career. So lots of women make the decision to give up their high salaries to take on less hours in order to raise children. This is a free choice.

However, the problem which no one can ignore is that it is women who are most likely to take time out of work to raise children. This is still a societal norm, and, while it doesn't mean that women are oppressed or marginalised, it does mean that there are things that employers can do to make the choice between having children and having a career a little less black and white.

These things are easy: state-provided, quality childcare, which would provide mothers with the freedom to continue their jobs while raising a family; more flexible working hours; and better access to paternity leave for fathers, which would help alleviate the expectation that women be the sole care givers for children.

So the pay gap question for women with children isn't about unfair discrimination or sexism in the workplace. The fact that women suffer pay gaps after childbirth should be part of a much wider conversation about the way in which women are still expected to take on the lion's share of childrearing. Under capitalism, there usually has to be a division of labour in households – like it or not, it's how the system works. Claiming that women are discriminated against on the basis of their gender ignores the underlying class dimensions and bigger problems that the exploitation of labour under a capitalist system raises. If the only thing wrong with women at work was that they're women, then why are some women billionaires and some women street sweepers? By focusing on gender, feminists, a bigger much more complex and important conversation about class, wealth, education and inequality in relation to society's resources. All of which have nothing to do with sex or gender.

We need a conversation about how to make working life better for everyone. Feminists' desire to paint women as subject to a mythical pay gap and at a disadvantage doesn't only ignore some key facts – it also mystifies the reality of the capitalist system, and instead blames all injustice on the intangible spectre of 'the patriarchy'.

The real trap of the glass ceiling

In her concession speech after the 2008 presidential election, Hillary Clinton declared: 'Although we weren't able to shatter that highest, hardest glass ceiling this time, thanks to you, it's got about 18million cracks in it, and the light is shining through like never before, filling us all with the hope and the sure knowledge that the path will be a little easier next time.'[55]

This speech would turn out to be extremely important for the next step in Clinton's political career. During her 2008 presidential campaign, she made it clear that she was not running on the basis of her gender, but on her merit as a presidential candidate. She did not want to be defined by the fact that she was a woman running against a man.

This drastically changed in 2016. Launching her campaign with

---

[55]   Clinton, Hillary, 'Hillary Clinton Endorses Barack Obama', 7 June 2008, *New York Times*, (Online)

the hashtag #GrandmaKnowsBest, Clinton's recent stab at being president was centred around the fact that she was female. On the popular US chat show, *Ellen,* she told the crowd: 'I'm not asking people to vote for me because I'm a woman, but if you vote for somebody on the merits, one of my merits is I'm a woman, and I think that makes a big difference in today's world.' Quite a u-turn.

There is a tendency for female politicians to present themselves as bringing a 'woman's touch' to politics. The infamous hug between Scottish National Party leader Nicola Sturgeon, Plaid Cymru leader Leanne Wood and Green Party leader Natalie Bennett, at the end of one of the televised leaders' debates during the 2015 UK General Election, was hailed by commentators as a progressive moment – indicative of a desire for a new 'cuddlier politics'. Clinton played the same game. In a biographical video used during her campaign, she was portrayed as vulnerable, emotional and in touch with her past, in a bid to convince Americans that, this time, she was the one they should vote for. Why? Because she wasn't just running as a Democrat, but as a 'wife, mom, grandma'.

All Clinton's claims about breaking the glass ceiling, and wanting to free women from the imagined shackles of their gender, ring hollow now. In fact, in promoting what came to be known as 'vagina voting' – voting for Clinton because she was a woman – Clinton's feminist campaign breathed life back into a reactionary depiction of women. In celebrating the fact that she was a woman, and a cuddly, warm, soft-hearted Grandma figure, Clinton's supporters rehabilitated all the old stereotypes of women: that we're kinder than men, that we're more gentle-hearted. That having a woman president would magically bring peace, love and harmony to politics.

The vast majority of contemporary feminists backed Hillary

Clinton. Why? It wasn't because Clinton had any radical policies which would make a material difference to women's lives but rather because having a female president was seen as radical in itself. Before the votes were cast, Lena Dunham angrily responded to criticism of so-called vagina voting. 'Accusing women of supporting Hillary just because she's female is misogynistic BS', Dunham wrote on one of her social-media accounts. Jessica Valenti, shared Dunham's opinion: 'Only in a sexist society would women be told that caring about representation at the highest levels of government is wrong.'[56] Both Dunham and Valenti argued that women were voting for Clinton because her gender *was* a policy – a policy of electing more women into political positions. To say that women were simply voting without thinking about this fact was an act of misogyny, apparently.

This sisterhood sentiment did not last for long when Clinton lost the presidential election to Donald Trump. In fact, following the revelation that 53 per cent of white women voted for Trump, Dunham and others started to attack women for being unintelligent or misled. 'It's painful to know that white women, so unable to see the unity of female identity, so unable to look past their violent privilege, and so inoculated with hate for themselves, showed up to the polls for him, too' said Dunham.[57] 'It is impossible to be feminist and not be appalled by the complicity of women in their own oppression', wrote *Guardian* journalist and feminist Suzanne Moore.[58] Women who voted for Trump are 'like slaves fluffing the pillows of their master's rocking chair on his porch

[56]   Valenti, Jessica, 'Hillary Clinton supporters: it is OK to care about gender on the ballot', 15 January 2016, *Guardian,* (Online)

[57]   Dunham, Lena, 'Don't Agonize, Organize', 11 November 2016, *Lenny,* (Online)

[58]   Moore, Suzanne, 'Why did women vote for Trump? Because misogyny is not a male-only attribute', 16 November 2016, *Guardian,* (Online)

as he shouts abuse at them', wrote Irish journalist Una Mullally.[59] Apparently the only reason women voted for Trump is because they were unthinkingly controlled by internalised misogyny – they were unable to make conscious, rational decisions. Those who voted for Clinton, on the other hand, they were smart, intelligent thinking women.

This is where identity politics leads – down an ugly, patronising, insulting road. That middle-class feminist writers like Dunham, Valenti, Moore and Mullally feel they have the right to denigrate the political decisions of millions of women is astounding. And it is evidence of how shallow and unthinking Clinton's feminist support was. The elephant in the room during Clinton's campaign was that she had no meaningful policies for women. She had the support of Planned Parenthood but had no plans to make abortion free and easily accessible for women. She profited from being a grandma but gave no concrete plans for childcare provision or better provision of maternity leave. She was all talk – she was running on her identity, not her politics.

So what glass ceiling was Clinton attempting to break? The fact that so much was made of the symbolism of a female president speaks to the emptiness of the narrative around smashing that ceiling. It's become a phrase used to capture the idea that women live in a society that is against them. Feminists need this fantastical ceiling, because it traps underneath it the idea that women are still subject to sexism, that life is worse for women. In this way, feminists still have a purpose.

That large numbers of America women rejected Clinton speaks to a positive new move against contemporary feminism. Though Trump will be no hero for freedom, let alone women's

59   Mullally, Una, 'Failed by white women – the undoing of Hillary Clinton', 9 November 2016, *Irish Times*, (Online)

freedom, in their rejection of Clinton's identity-politics driven campaign, American women proved that they have no time for this mythical glass ceiling. That they're much more interested in what they perceive to be the fragile ground holding them up. However much you might disagree with Trump, voters favoured the sexist who talked about material change over the grandma who talked about pretend glass.

The thing about equality...

Gender quotas have been a major focus of many over the past 20 years. In 1997, the number of female MPs doubled overnight, with Labour electing 101 women to parliament. The nickname 'Blair's Babes', given to the new intake by the *Daily Mail*, stuck. Twenty years on, and UK political parties are still fretting over the lack of skirt in parliament. This is despite the fact that of those 101 new female employees, not one woman has explicitly argued for political change which would improve women's lives or further women's freedom.

So why are we so obsessed with the idea of equal representation, if it so often proves to be useless? What is it about being a woman that guarantees a politician will believe in women's freedom? Mention Margaret Thatcher and feminists will often roll their eyes and yet she sums up the fact that women politicians don't always favour women's freedom. The same can be said for the UK's current prime minister, Theresa May, who certainly has no plans to campaign for abortion rights or access to childcare. What about Kellyanne Conway, Trump's counsellor, who mocked the women's march against Trump in January and said she 'didn't see the point of it'? These female politicians and public figures are not feminist by default – and simply having them involved in politics dosen't make life any better for women. So why do feminists continue to argue that an injection of lipstick will make politics better?

Clementine Ford, author and prominent Australian feminist, told the *Guardian,* 'to redress the imbalance that women are experiencing, men have to lose something, and not just figuratively but literally. They have to give up some of their power.'[60] 'It's actual physics, let's make the room bigger', she continued, 'but the reality is you can't make the parliament larger, so men have to give up their seats if we really want equality'. Like the actress Emma Watson's UN campaign 'He for She', feminists are encouraging men to give up the physical and metaphorical space they occupy in public life, and make way for women.

There are two issues with this approach to women in politics. Firstly, it undermines democracy. MPs are not simply elected on the basis of what the party needs – they must be the right person for the job and be elected by the people. Secondly, there is nothing more insulting than suggesting that a woman should get her job on the basis of her gender over her merit. It would be very hard to find a self-respecting woman who would accept a job simply to make up a quota, rather than for the fact that she is the right person to hold that particular role.

Ford's comments came at a time when quotas were a big topic of debate in Australia. Former prime minister John Howard caused outrage when he said there would never be 50/50 gender representation in politics: 'Women play a significantly greater part of fulfilling the caring role in our communities which inevitably place some limits on their capacity'[61], he argued. Howard was denounced by feminists as a misogynist.

[60]   Delaney, Brigid '"There's something really toxic with the way men bond in Australia"', 28 September 2016, *Guardian,* (Online)

[61]   Burke, Liz, 'John Howard: Women have 'limits on capacity' in politics', 7 September 2016, news.com, (Online)

Elena Jeffreys, a sex-worker and feminist commentator from Sydney, tweeted: 'John Howard you sexist moron. How do you keep yourself upright you are so stupid. I suppose we can blame your wife for care-giving you.'

Many Australian feminists came out to denounce Howard. But his comments were not a million miles away from feminists' own argument for equal gender representation. The common phrase used by feminists to describe parliamentary politics, in Australia, the US and the UK, is 'pale, male and stale'. Women, feminists argue, bring a loving, caring role to politics. In a campaign video for Hillary Clinton titled #ThisIsWhatMyRevolutionLooksLike, female celebrities celebrated the fact that women do politics by 'leading, by listening, communicating, collaborating, consensus building, and with love. Because that's how we women do it.'[62] Feminists and women calling for 50/50 representation argue that they want more women in politics because they're more caring, compassionate and loving, but they are appalled when someone like Howard suggests women play a caring role.

The feminisation of work

In the 1953 Doris Day musical *Calamity Jane*, Day and co-star Allyn Ann McLerie sing a number called 'A Woman's Touch'. 'A woman's touch can weave a spell, the kind of hocus pocus that she does so well', they sing. Of course, they're singing about housework – but the idea of women being different, more caring, more pernickety, more feminised, is there, albeit in a playful way. Far less playful and more problematic is contemporary feminists' desire to make real this crude characterisation of women.

---

[62] Vagianos, Alanna, 'Famous Women On Why A Woman President Is A "Revolution"', 25 July 2016, *Huffington Post,* (Online).

Since the 1970s, with legislation like the UK Sex Discrimination Act in 1975, the argument that work is a dangerous place for women has proliferated. Of course, in the 1970s and perhaps the 1980s, the workplace may well have been a rather unpleasant place for women – as sexism was, back then, a real thing. But was it dangerous? Did it stop women from wanting to enter the world of work? No.

Since then, contemporary feminists have made it their mission to paint public life, and work in general, as a danger to women. Women's worth is in danger from the gender pay gap, women's psychological wellbeing is in danger from leering bosses, and women's bodies are in danger from normalised workplace harassment.

And how do feminists respond to these so-called dangers? By inventing quotas to get more women into work – to equal out or combat the male danger. Not only is this insulting to any notion of what women can individually bring to the workplace, in terms of worth and skills – it also paints a false and worrying picture of the threats women face today. Forget the pay gap or sexist bosses – what will really put women off following a career is the fatalist approach of feminists who fearmonger about the dangers of public life.

The idea that women bring sugar and spice and all things nice to public life is most problematic when it comes to women in politics. What politics needs is big ideas – what women need is an individual who is willing to fight for those big ideas. Whether that's a man or a woman is irrelevant. The idea that seeing more women in politics will encourage more women to become politically active is insulting. This is the argument behind vagina voting: that you can only relate to someone politically if they mirror your identity.

If any government, tomorrow, kicked out half its men and elected women in their place, nothing would change. Female biology has no impact on politics – that an MP or a political representative is female makes no difference to their understanding of what women want from politics. You don't have to have had an abortion to know that women should have freedom over their own bodies. You don't have to have had kids to know that better childcare provision is a necessary requirement for most working mothers. A belief in women's freedom doesn't come naturally to women, it comes from a universal belief in humanity. The idea that an Oxbridge-educated female MP in a leafy suburb would automatically be able to relate to a single mother in Toxteth simply because they both have two X chromosomes is absurd.

If women want to change politics, they must argue for real change, not a makeover in parliament. By arguing for gender quotas and superficial attempts at making politics *seem* more equal, feminists are denigrating what it means to be a woman. If we believe that simply having more women in politics makes politics nicer and kinder and better, we're making a judgement about women – we are stereotyping women, limiting them of what they are capable of doing, instead of treating them as free-thinking individuals.

Radicals used to believe that the important things to fight for in terms of work were better wages, for both men and women, greater control over workers' freedom, and a better quality of working life for all. Feminists now actively encourage women to see their working lives through the prism of gender. This thwarts any real and meaningful change in people's working lives. If women are to see unemployment and job insecurity as related to gender, rather than as failures of our economic and political systems, doesn't that destroy any notion of solidarity and the possibility of organisations among working-class people. Feminists are encouraging the female factory worker to believe that she has nothing in common with and everything to fear from her male colleague. So when they both get laid off, there is no common ground from which to build a challenge. Feminists aren't radical: they're colluding with the bosses, they're atomising workers and destroying any notion of solidarity and organisation among working people.

What's holding back women in the workplace? It's not sexist bosses or arse-slapping colleagues, it's not even short maternity leave or lower wages. It's feminists' obsession with painting women as in need of a leg-up. Because the thing about equality is, unless you win it on your own terms, rather than pleading for it from a position of weakness, it comes to nothing.

5

AN END TO FEMINISM

When I was a gobby teenager, and later a wannabe student radical, feminism was still something a bit exotic. At school, feminism was something hairy women did, and, at university, it was something theoretical.

But today, in contrast, feminism is almost like a compulsory tick-box for young women. Celebrities climb over each other to 'come out' as feminists in the hope of a few headlines. When someone doesn't decide to take the F-label, they're slated for being either mistaken or misogynistic. It's the same for young girls. Even at school, feminism is pushed with equality initiatives and 'He for She' UN-sponsored PSHE lessons. Schoolchildren are taught how to be feminists. After the birth of her daughter, Nigerian novelist and outspoken feminist Chimamanda Ngozi Adichie published a 9,000-word 'feminist manifesto in 15 suggestions'. We have to teach our daughters how to be feminists, says Adichie, including by teaching them to read, 'be a full person' and to 'reject the idea of conditional female equality', or, as she puts it, 'Feminism Lite'.[63]

---

[63] Dahir, Abdi Latif, 'Chimamanda Adichie has 15 suggestions for how to raise a feminist child', 15 October 2016, *Quartz*, (Online)

Herein lies feminism's crucial problem: it's no longer a political movement. In fact, it hasn't been for years. Ever since feminism became about how women should feel, what women should wear and how women should see themselves, it has turned into an identity. Feminism is the original and most pure form of identity politics.

This means it has no end in sight – it has no goals. If we have to learn how to raise feminists, and grow up to be feminists, and teach our daughters how to become feminists, where is the time or the space to fight for what feminism is supposed to be about – women's freedom? How do feminists see the future? Will feminism always be there? Because, if it is, then that necessitates the continual stalling of women's freedom – why would you need a movement which prioritises women's political issues if women were truly equal? Instead of being a means to an end, feminism as a means to liberating women – feminism has become an end in itself. It's defunct. It's fake. It's utterly meaningless.

Identity politics is anti politics. There is nothing inherently political about emotion or subjective experience or feelings – all of which identity politics has at its core. A truly radical and progressive politics is one which seeks to engage a universal outlook, one that celebrates individuality in the context of a strong collective.

Identity politics refutes both these things. It denigrates any sense of individuality by claiming that people are defined not by what they do but by the nature of their gender, skin colour or their sexuality. And, more importantly, it denigrates any potential for collective or universal thinking by arguing that we can never transcend subjective experience – no two people with different identities can share the same political outlook. It's fundamentally impossible, identity politics argues, for a white straight woman like myself to engage in, or understand, the political desires of a black gay man – because how would I know what it's like to live as a black gay man? The terms 'mansplaining' or 'male privilege' express a similar outlook – how can men understand what it's like to be a woman? How could a man argue for abortion rights better than a woman, when he doesn't have a uterus? In this way, any notion of political solidarity or forming a public collective around a political idea becomes impossible. Politics is no longer about the external (society, the public, the people), but instead comes to be focused on the internal (feelings, identity, self-worth). Feminism is identity politics, and it has no place in a universal and progressive fight for women's liberation.

The right kind of woman

Adichie's list for raising a feminist is interesting - it's also highly unoriginal. Over the past 10 years, feminists have made a living out of writing how-to guides on feminism, telling women how to feel and how to act. Here's a short list of some of the top feminists how-to manuals on the market right now:

Full Frontal Feminism: A Young Woman's Guide to Why Feminism Matters by Jessica Valenti (2007)

How to Be a Woman by Caitlin Moran (2011)

How to Build a Girl by Caitlin Moran (2014)

Not That Kind of Girl: A Young Woman Tells You What She's Learned by Lena Dunham (2014)

Bad Feminist by Roxane Gay (2014)

Unspeakable Things: Sex, Lies and Revolution by Laurie Penny (2014)

Do It Like a Woman ... and Change the World by Caroline Criado-Perez (2015)

Girl Up by Laura Bates (2016)

These books and essays seek to instruct women on how to be, in feminists' eyes, better women. The clue is in the title – these feminists are literally using the language of self-help and DIY literature to condition women into thinking a certain way. Through obsequious anecdotes and painful mini-manifestos, these feminist authors want to carve out a type of 'good' woman.

This good woman is a feminist – she likes to hate the patriarchy, she's aware of her oppression and, most importantly, she loves herself. She sometimes shaves her legs, but never because society wants her to. She voted for Hillary Clinton or would if she could. She talks about her private life in public to counteract the pressure put on women to conform to an ideal image. She rails against the depiction of women in the media but gleefully accepts any public face time on issues related to periods, fat-shaming or sexual harassment. She doesn't go to clubs or Magaluf because that's where boorish men go, and she wears short skirts, not for her looks but for her sisters, to prove that she can.

In short, this 'good woman' – who coincidentally bears an extraordinary resemblance to many contemporary feminists today – is a middle-class bore. Feminists want women to sign up to playing a role. Women must be ever vigilant for signs of sexism, they must build themselves up to be feminists, they must wear the badge with glee.

So, what constitutes a bad woman? According to contemporary feminism, bad women have sex for fun, and sometimes they do it drunk. Bad women bottlefeed their children instead of freeing their nipples at every cafe and cornershop. Bad women get their boobs out because they're getting paid for it, or because their boyfriend likes them. Bad women voted for Trump and Brexit and think about politics rather than identity. Bad women feel comfortable enough in their own body to shrug off comments and remarks made by men without it making them scared. Bad women don't go crying to the authorities when someone shouts at them they shout back.

Bad women, then, are normal women. Most women do not adhere to contemporary feminism. We don't agonise about being scarred after a one-night stand, we put it down to a bad decision or a great night. We don't tweet every time someone says something rude to us, we deal with it there and then. Most women are normal, rational human beings who don't feel the need to 'do it like a' anything. Most women want politics to be the pursuit of greater freedom, not a feel-good sorority.

But this patronising advice to women is nothing original. Women have always had a helping hand in how to act and what to do. Contemporary feminists are merely borrowing from history, and giving their own spin on what has been a long tradition of panicking over women's role in public. Here's a short list of some old texts contemporary feminism is mirroring:

The Lady's Guide to Perfect Gentility by Emily Thornwell (1857)

American Etiquette and Rules of Politeness by *Walter R. Houghton (1883)*

Etiquette of Good Society by Lady Colin Campbell (1893)

What Can a Woman Do by Mrs M.L. Rayne (1893)

A Word to Women by Mrs Humphry (1898)

Woman in Girlhood, Wifehood, Motherhood: Her Responsibilities and Her Duties at All Periods of Life; a Guide in the Maintenance of Her Own Health and That of Her Children by Myer Solis-Cohen (1906)

The vulnerable woman

The offshoot of contemporary feminism's campaign to protect women is that women are now seen as vulnerable.

Human resources departments will have equal-opportunities policies, which name women as a minority identity group in need of protection. In the UK, off the back of the Equality Act, women have become a legally protected section of the population – we are literally, by law, painted as more vulnerable than men.

Not only is this a false depiction of women's strength and ability – it is also a dire and depressing outlook for feminists to call their own. Whatever happened to Rosie Riveter? That image of a woman, sleeves rolled up, ready to take on the world? Even though she was originally a glorified version of working women during the Second World War, she became known as a symbol of women's empowerment. With a scowl and muscles showing, she's the antithesis of the idea of the vulnerable woman. Why have feminists gone against this depiction? Why is it controversial to say that women are rough, tough and ugly enough to be treated the same way as men – and be able to deal with the trials and tribulations of life as well as men?

We often hear the phrase 'women and girls'. Or 'End violence against women and girls'. The 'Women and Girls Initiative'. 'Women and girls network.' The *Guardian* has its own category for news about women and girls. One of the UN's projects is titled ' empowering women and girls'. 'This has been a bad week for girls and women', read one recent *Financial Times* article.[64]

On the one hand, feminists argue that using the word 'girls' to describe women is, as the website Everyday Sexism puts it, 'sexist as hell', but on the other they seem perfectly comfortable with lumping girls and women together. This is interesting, because the continual grouping of women and girls says something important about the way society views women. That the distinction between

---

[64]   Smith, Kerry, 'This has been a bad week for women and girls', 25 January 2017, *Financial Times*, (Online)

child and adult has become so happily blurred when it comes to women should be a warning sign: women are now assumed to have the same needs as children.

This is most tangible when it comes to mental health. In no other area of political discussion are women more infantilised, patronised and insulted. Women are reportedly more at risk from self-harm and depression due to the pressures put on them by society. This doesn't include the struggle to make rent, feed kids or find a job. Instead, feminists claim that the issues women face are things like pressure from social media and the depiction of women's bodies. In other words, women and girls suffer from low self esteem.

So, what do we want, as women who want to change the world and be equal players in public life? Do we want to be portrayed as being on the brink of mental illness? Or as children? Or as a vulnerable identity group, in need or protection and special care? Or do we want to scrap all of that and give two fingers to playing the damsel in distress? Do we want to fight for a definition of womanhood that means strength, individuality and freedom? Should we tell our daughters to be tough-necked, hard-skinned and mean in the face of adversity? Or should we encourage them to melt into the background like wall flowers, forever in the debt of some policy or some authority's helping hand to get on in the world?

What women want

This is why feminism must end: because women have too much to lose for it to continue, and too much to gain from a serious political movement that could come in its place. What contemporary feminists can't grasp, what haunts them in their

Islington townhouses, is that their middle-class girls' sorority is short-lived. Women don't want to play by the rules of a girls' club which seeks to instruct them on how to behave, how to have sex, how to view their place in society and how to think politically. A club which treats them like helpless children. Women want freedom – to have fun, and to think independently.

None of this is possible under this patronising and selective clique. Contemporary feminism increasingly looks like a bunch of snooty and anti-working class media commentators, hell bent on making headlines about bullshit stories. They hate the fact that working-class women want nothing to do with them, that a young girl in Tottenham will have far more in common with the boy who lives next door to her than she will with a *Guardian* journalist who happens to be female. They hate that politics is about more than pubic hair and whether or not pop songs are sexist. They're infinitely scared of what women want, because the majority of women want them to get lost.

Any self-respecting, free-thinking woman worth her salt will demand the right to think what she likes and say what she thinks. Feminism thwarts women's free speech, it thwarts women's free thought, and it denies women the right to self determine and form their own political consciousness. Feminism is child's play – it's politics for show.

In his *Theses on Feuerbach*[65], Karl Marx (neither a feminist nor a woman) wrote: 'The philosophers have only interpreted the world, in various ways; the point is to change it.' It's time that women took a stand and demanded a political movement that changed the world, rather than one which is content with carping from the sidelines.

[65]   Marx, Karl, *Theses On Feuerbach*, Progress Publishers, 1969

Young women are more politically aware and radically inclined than ever before. What a wonderful opportunity ripe with possibility this is. Women need a political movement to secure the remaining freedoms withheld from us – our bodily autonomy and our position in society as equals in the home and at work. We need to argue for abortion rights, childcare, material changes to our lives. Women need humanism, universalism, freedom – a political movement which demands all and more, which doesn't prescribe rules or regulations but breaks open the possibilities of the world for women. Contemporary feminism, as it stands, will never deliver on these goals.

This is because, feminism is not a political movement – it's an identity. And what a boring idea that we should all be carbon copies of Caitlin Moran or Harriet Harman. No, women want freedom, and that's something which has to be won through battle and hardship and bare-faced demands for independence. Women need to insist that they be treated like independent individuals, that they be free to choose their own lifestyle and their own life choices, free from state intervention and legal contestation.

But most of all, women must understand that their fight for freedom does not stand isolated from history or context, that it is not linked to their identity or subjective experience, but rather is a universal struggle for freedom, and that it has an endpoint. There should be a point in the future in which it's unheard of to be a feminist, or even to be someone who fights for women's rights – because we'll have won that fight.

So feminists, take note, your days are numbered. Free-thinking women don't want to be bound by your rules – we want fun, freedom and an end to your patronising, illiberal feminism. It's time for women to get serious about liberation, and fight for their right to live as fully free and autonomous individuals.

The end of feminism spells the beginning of a movement for women's liberation – bring it on.

sp!ked

Launched in 2001, as Britain's first online-only current-affairs mag, *spiked* is a metaphorical missile against misanthropy.

It's the publication that puts the case for human endeavour, intellectual risk-taking, exploration, excellence in learning and art, and freedom of speech with no ifs and buts, against the myriad miserabilists who would seek to wrap humans in red tape, dampen down our daring, restrain our thoughts, and police our speech.

spiked is a fan of reason, liberty, progress, economic growth, choice, conviction and thought experiments about the future, and not so big on eco-miserabilism, identikit politicians, nostalgia, dumbing down and determinism.

We echo Saint-Simon, who said: 'The golden age, which a blind tradition has always placed in the past, is really in front of us.' spiked is all about laying the ground for, and having a pop at the enemies of, that still-to-come golden age for humankind.

Edited by Brendan O'Neill, and run by a tiny team of underpaid staff, *spiked* publishes Monday to Friday, covering everything from politics and war to sex, sport and art.

www.spiked-online.com

Lightning Source UK Ltd.
Milton Keynes UK
UKHW01f1823290618
325011UK00001B/117/P